SKETCHING
FOR ARCHITECTURE + INTERIOR DESIGN

to mark, samantha + matthew

Published in 2015 by
Laurence King Student & Professional
An imprint of Quercus Editions Ltd
Carmelite House
50 Victoria Embankment
London EC4Y 0DZ

An Hachette UK company

Reprinted 2016, 2017, 2018, 2019, 2020, 2021

A catalogue record for this book is available from the
British Library.

ISBN: 978-1-78067-564-0

Design: TwoSheds Design
Senior Editor: Peter Jones

Printed and bound in China
by Toppan Leefung

SKETCHING

FOR ARCHITECTURE + INTERIOR DESIGN

Stephanie Travis

Laurence King Publishing

CONTENTS

INTRODUCTION

WHY SKETCH?

Drawing is truly a tool for seeing. To draw an object, interior, or building, you have to look at the subject in a new way. You are forced to pause and scrutinize, as drawing requires another way of thinking, shifting into a deeper realm that encompasses elements such as shape, form, texture, rhythm, composition, and light. When you have developed your drawing skills, the finer details of a space—key features that you may not previously have noticed—will be revealed to you. Freehand drawing allows viewers to see in a way they never have before. The sketching process is a means of expanding your creativity and awakening your senses.

THE CONCEPT

The consistent thread throughout this book are my freehand sketches, shown as a series of steps to demonstrate the underlying concept—that an understanding of the *process* of creating meaningful sketches is more important than the end drawing itself.

The cumulative process of sketching always begins with studying the subject, whether it be a chair, an interior, or an entire building. It is about drawing what you see, not what you think you see, or what you already know as a chair, interior, or building. Think of it as seeing the subject for the first time. Each exercise illustrates a different facet of this concept of seeing. As you move through the steps of each exercise, you will explore each subject in a new way, gaining the experience and confidence to create expressive, thoughtful sketches that convey your personal interpretation of the subject.

HOW TO USE THE BOOK

It is intended that you start from the beginning of this book and work through the exercises as the scale and complexity increases. Chapter 1 (Furniture + Lighting) begins with small-scale objects; Chapter 2 (Interiors) expands into more complex spaces; and Chapter 3 (Architecture) focuses on larger-scale buildings. Each exercise within the three sections incorporates many sketches for reference, with examples of modern designs of furniture and lighting, interiors, and architecture by significant modern and contemporary designers and architects. The name of the object, interior space, or building; the architect or designer; the year of design or completion; and the location of the interior or building are provided at the end of each exercise. You will select your own furniture and lighting, interiors, or buildings to sketch. Subjects may be viewed in three dimensions (from life) or two dimensions (from photographs, periodicals, etc.). What is important is to select subjects that you find challenging and inspiring.

The example sketches were all drawn in ink, and I suggest that you also use ink, at least at first—this forces you to study carefully the subject you are drawing, knowing that any mistakes cannot simply be erased. These exercises are just a starting point. To develop your practice further, you can repeat them with more complex, detailed objects and using different media (e.g. graphite/pencil, charcoal, etc.). But, whether you use ink, pencil, or a combination of both, the exercises provide a methodology for studying your subject and drawing what you see. It is not about laboriously crafting perfect technical drawings.

The three sections cover topics such as layering, perspective, repetition, pattern, foreground + background, negative space, multiple viewpoints, shade + shadow, and composition. The steps within each exercise build upon each other so that you achieve a thorough exploration of the subject before producing a complete sketch. You should redraw exercises at each step,

as the key to improvement is practice. Although each exercise ends with a final sketch, the focus of this book is on the experience and process of sketching, more than on the finished work.

MATERIALS

To complete the exercises in this book, you will need the following: a sketchbook, three ink pens, and a selection of professional markers in gray. I use a basic 9" x 12" wire-bound sketchbook with standard white paper and the pens/markers as illustrated and specified opposite. I purchase the thin- and medium-width pens from office supply stores; other supplies are from art specialty stores. Ultimately, the brand of pen is not the important factor; it is what you do with it.

As you continue to sketch, you should experiment with different types and styles of pens. To begin, it is important only that you have three pen widths and a selection of cool gray markers, although you can also experiment with warm gray markers.

Note that throughout this book I have predominantly used the medium pen. Wherever a thin pen, thick pen, or the gray markers were used in a sketch, this will be specified. If there is no notation in the text, the sketch was drawn with the medium pen. Although the markers will be used to explore an understanding of shade/shadow, many of the exercises use the varied gray values of the markers to explore other elements—such as contrasting shapes, planes, and forms or to study how elements recede or protrude.

The tools I use:

Thin pen: Uniball Super Ink pen in black.

Medium pen: Paper Mate Flair M pen in black.

Thick pen: Faber-Castell Pitt Artist pen B in black.

Markers: Prismacolor Premier markers in cool gray ranging from 10 percent (the lightest) to 100 percent (black).

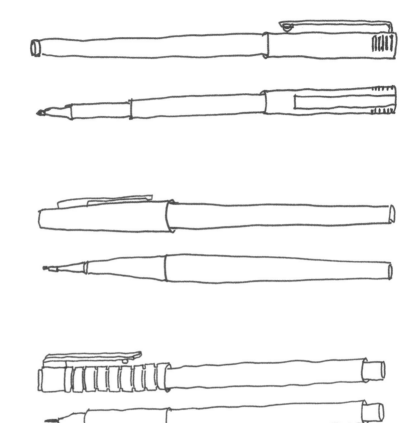

PEN WARM-UP

Once you have your sketching supplies, it is important to explore your thin, medium, and thick pens. This warm-up will help you to understand line thickness and quality, as well as practice hand and wrist control.

1.

Draw a series of lines with very thin spacing between them. First, use your thin pen, then your medium pen, and finally your thick pen.

2.

Repeat, increasing the spacing between your lines.

3.

Draw the lines with even wider spacing between your lines.

MARKER WARM-UP

It is also important to understand the quality of your markers. Most professional markers have a tip on each end, thin and thick.

1.

Draw a series of thinly spaced lines, using the thin tip starting at 10 percent gray and moving in numeric order to 20 percent gray, 30 percent gray, etc., until you reach 90 percent.

2.

Repeat using the thick tip of your marker.

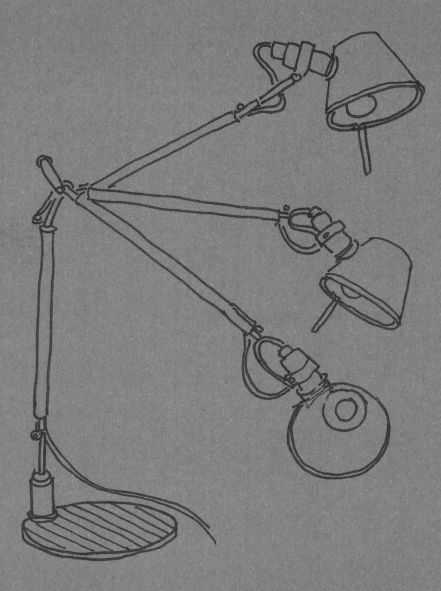

1.
FURNITURE + LIGHTING

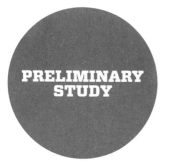

PRELIMINARY STUDY

The purpose of this exercise is to examine the overall form as well as the unique details of an object while exploring varied pen thicknesses. Understanding the quality and output of your thin, medium, and thick pens is important, as the pens become important communicators in the sketching process. In this example the light fixture has many interesting details, including its ability to be adjusted by rotating or tilting. These qualities are captured with quick studies that explore many different elements of the fixture.

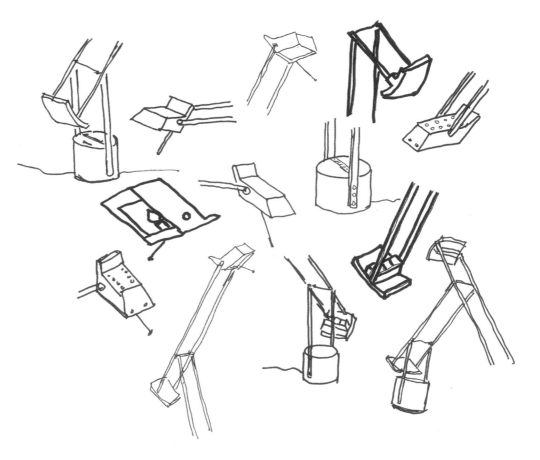

1.

Select a light fixture Alternate between using your thin, medium, and thick pens to fill an entire sketchbook page with studies of your fixture. Move around the fixture to record what you can see from different angles. Zoom in to compelling details of a larger fixture.

2.

Using each pen (thin, medium, and thick),
sketch the light fixture in its entirety.

LIGHTING SPECIFICATION
....

Tizio floor lamp
Richard Sapper | 2009

ABSTRACTION

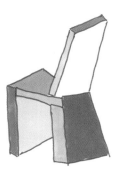

This exercise uses abstraction as a sketching tool to examine the sculptural qualities of a chair. Simplifying the chair into a series of individual shapes helps you to understand the overall form more clearly. Note that the term shape refers to a two-dimensional element, such as a plane, while the term form refers to a three-dimensional element, such as a box. An abstraction study is an effective way to study an object, as it translates a complex form into flat, basic shapes and provides a thorough understanding of the design.

1.

Select three chairs Abstract each chair into simple shapes, similar to building blocks. With your markers, use varied intensities of gray (e.g. percentages of 10, 30, 50, 70, 90) to define each shape by rendering the planes with contrasting percentages. To render means to fill in. Rendered/filled in areas on an architectural drawing may also be referred to as poché. If a plane is rendered with 10 percent gray, use 30 percent or higher for the adjoining plane to provide contrast.

2.

Sketch the form of the chair, using your thick pen. A line drawing in a broad, heavy stroke emphasizes the unique form of the chair.

3.

While line drawings capture the overall form of an object, rendering the material conveys an additional layer of information. Add the materials of your chairs to your drawings. In this example the chairs on the left and center were designed using sheets of corrugated cardboard that are glued or laminated together, producing a linear texture. To express this texture a thin pen is used to represent the edges of the cardboard. As each layer of cardboard is very thin and the lines are close together, a medium pen would read too dark and dominate the sketch. The chair on the right comprises two-inch strips of maple wood that are bent and woven to create the form. Here a medium pen is used for both the outline and the woven texture, as the strips are significantly wider than the cardboard edges in the previous chairs.

CHAIR SPECIFICATIONS from left
....
Easy Edges chair
Frank Gehry I 1972
....
Wiggle chair
Frank Gehry I 1972
....
Cross Check chair
Frank Gehry I 1992

NEGATIVE STUDY

This exercise focuses on the space around and within an object, often referred to as negative space. Examining the voids that occur between individual elements of a larger object will help you to understand and sketch the object accurately. Continued practise using your three pens will help you to control your pen movement. A successful sketch is drawn with a fluid, confident line with the pen touching the paper. Avoid the mini-strokes that occur when a pen is lifted off the paper too many times while drawing a line. This creates a scratchy appearance that detracts from the drawing. Further use of your markers will provide more familiarity with the gray-scale values.

1.

Select three table lamps with shades
To get the most out of this exercise, select lamps with contrasting base forms, like the ones chosen for this example. Draw the base of the first lamp with an imaginary box around it and hatch the interior shape that occurs between the lamp base and the edges of the box. Repeat this two more times so that there are three negative-space drawings for the lamp. Use thin, medium, and thick pens to draw evenly spaced lines within each drawing. Repeat this exercise for the other two lamps.

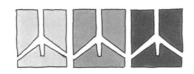

2.

Repeat step 1, using markers in three different gray values/intensities to render the shapes. For more contrast, use 10 percent, 50 percent, and 90 percent; for less contrast, use 20 percent, 40 percent, and 60 percent. Avoid using black (100 percent).

3.

Sketch each lamp, including the shade, with a medium pen. Use the negative-space exercises as a guide to draw the base.

LIGHTING SPECIFICATIONS from left

Cindy table lamp
Ferruccio Laviani I 2009

Lumiere XXL table lamp
Rodolfo Dordoni I 1990

Stilt table lamp
Blu Dot I 2010

POSITIVE STUDY

We studied negative space in the previous exercise. Now the focus is on the inverse, referred to as positive space. This is the actual space that the form takes up. Concentrating on the object itself and the overall shapes that create the form is another way to study an object.

1.

Select three table lamps Use thin, medium, and thick pens to draw evenly spaced lines within the lamp form. Repeat this process for each lamp.

2.

Repeat step 1, using markers in three different gray values/intensities to define the form of the lamp. Do not outline the subject. In this example the values used are 20 percent, 50 percent, and 80 percent.

3.

Sketch the lamps with a medium pen.

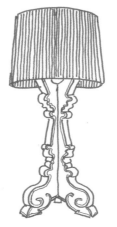

LIGHTING SPECIFICATIONS from left

Miss Sissi table lamp
Philippe Starck I 1991

Castore table lamp
Michele De Lucchi I 2003

Bourgie table lamp
Ferruccio Laviani I 2003

MIRROR IMAGE

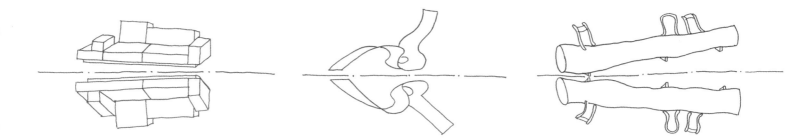

This exercise explores the idea of reflection. Sketching the mirror image of an object is another way to study it. Instead of drawing a piece of furniture, or what one thinks of as a piece of furniture, this exercise abstracts the object into a sculptural form, so that the emphasis is not on the drawing itself, but on the study of the form.

1.

Select three wide seating pieces (e.g. sofa, chaise, bench) With a dashed line, define the ground-floor plane. Draw your object above the line. While looking only at your sketch of the object (not the object in real life), draw your object mirrored below the line. Study the negative space between your object and the ground plane in order to position the piece below the line. Repeat this exercise for the two other seating pieces you have chosen.

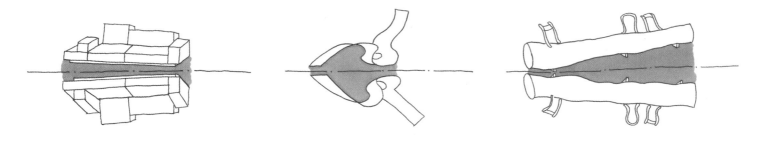

2.

Use a gray marker to define the shape of
the negative space that results between
your objects and the dashed ground plane.

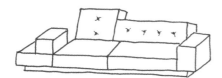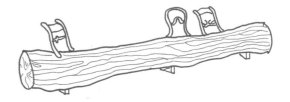

3.

Draw each of your seating pieces, adding
interior details—like (from left to right)
the button tufting, polished bronze
reflections, and natural wood grain
included in these examples.

FURNITURE SPECIFICATIONS from left

Polder sofa
Hella Jongerius I 2005

After Spring chaise longue
Ron Arad I 1992

Tree Trunk bench
Jurgen Bey I 1999

GUIDELINES

This exercise underlines the importance of setting up guidelines and continues to build upon the idea of negative space. Creating guidelines and emphasizing the space around/within an object provides a greater understanding of the subject.

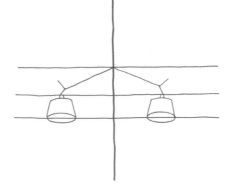

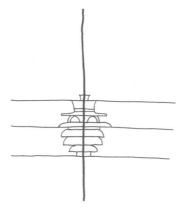

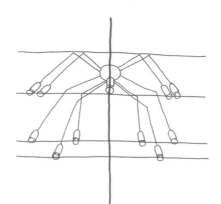

1.

Select three symmetrical hanging light fixtures Use your thick pen to draw the centerline of each light fixture and your medium pen to draw the horizontal lines that define the major elements of the fixtures. Draw simplified versions of your fixtures.

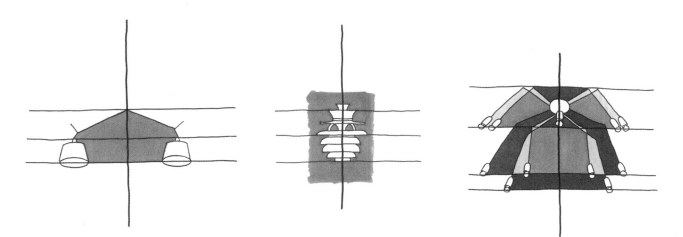

2.

Sketch the negative space between or around each fixture. In the example, the pendant on the left has a straightforward void shape. The pendant in the center is a large central form and the negative space occurs mainly around the fixture, so an imaginary box is drawn around the object and the negative space rendered. The pendant on the right is more complicated as it has many individual voids. Therefore, it is rendered in varied gray intensities to differentiate the negative spaces.

3.

Draw each fixture in its entirety.

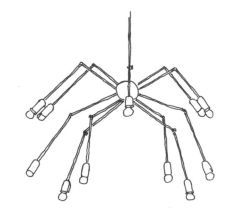

LIGHTING SPECIFICATIONS from left

Tolomeo Double Shade pendant lamp
Michele De Lucchi & Giancarlo Fassina I 1987

PH Snowball pendant lamp
Poul Henningsen I 1924

Double Octopus pendant lamp
Seyhan Özdemir & Sefer Çaglar I 2005

LAYERS

Parts of an object that protrude toward the viewer are closer and it is often possible to perceive them in greater detail. Parts that recede are farther away and therefore tend to be less clearly visible. It is important to delineate these elements before sketching an intricate object. Sketch protruding elements more tightly or draw them with a thicker pen. Conversely, represent receding elements with a looser sketch or draw them with a thinner pen. This principle is most evident when drawing interiors but can also be applied to complex furniture and lighting. This exercise shows how to analyze an object comprising many individual elements in order to determine how to represent its protruding and receding parts in a sketch.

1.

Select three hanging light fixtures with layered elements Create an abstract line drawing of the light fixture. Number the elements in terms of their distance from the viewer, starting with the number 1 for the element that is closest.

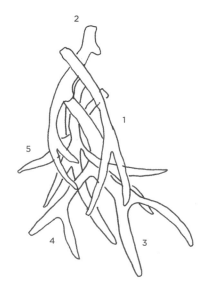

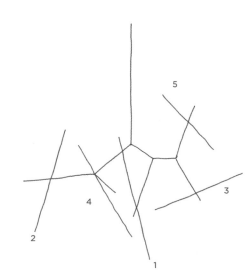

2.

Create a line drawing that focuses on a significant aspect of the light fixture, or what needs the most exploration. The focus may be different for each light. In this example it varies from the glass globe (left) to the linear fixture that holds the bulb (center) to the tightly wound antlers (right). Use the numbers from the previous exercise to determine the percentage of gray in which to render the elements with your markers; darkest gray for elements labeled 1, medium gray for 2, lighter gray for 3, and so on. This principle—elements that are closer are darker, elements that are farther away are lighter—is an important aspect of sketching that will be used when drawing more complex, larger-scale subjects such as interiors and buildings.

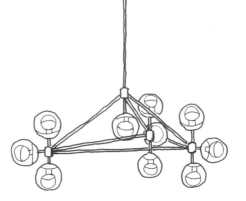

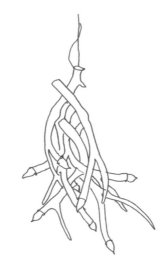

3.

Sketch your light fixtures in their entirety. Be mindful to draw overlapping elements in order of proximity to the viewer, with closer elements drawn first. If you were doing this sketch in pencil, you could erase overlapping lines. However, working with pen encourages you to think about the order in which the elements occur before drawing the subject.

LIGHTING SPECIFICATIONS from left

Modo chandelier (3-sided)
Jason Miller I 2009

Agnes chandelier (10 lights)
Lindsey Adelman I 2010

Superordinate Antler chandelier (4 antlers)
Jason Miller I 2003

1.

Select three benches Outline the basic form of your bench and use markers to render the sides of the block with varied gray intensity to emphasize the different planes.

PERSPECTIVE BASICS

The concept of this book is to draw what you see. However, the basic laws of perspective—which are covered throughout the exercises in this book—are key to understanding what it is that you see in three dimensions, which in turn will improve your sketching skills. Viewed in a space, objects recede to a vanishing point (hereafter referred to as the VP); this is the farthest point that the eye can see. When viewing an object of some length, you will notice the lines begin (very slightly) to taper to this imaginary point. This is difficult to make out in smaller furniture such as a stool, but is discernible in more lengthy pieces such as benches—and clearly evident in larger-scale subjects such as interiors and buildings.

When viewing an object straight on, there will be one VP; when viewing the object from a corner, there will be two VPs. Complex objects, interiors, and buildings (specifically with curved or angled elements) can have more VPs. However, for the exercises in this book (with the exception of the Multi-point Perspective exercise, see page 106), we will limit ourselves to one- and two-point perspectives.

For this exercise a brief explanation on perspective is adequate. The idea is to look very closely at your object to get the information you need for this sketch.

2.

Draw the benches with arrows indicating the direction of the lines toward the VP(s). In this example the bottom-left bench is viewed straight-on as a one-point perspective, so that there is only one VP. The other two benches are viewed looking at a corner as a two-point perspective, so that there are two VPs (one to the left of the corner and one to the right of the corner).

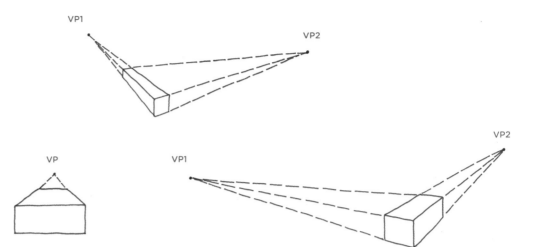

3.

Sketch simplified versions of the overall forms of your benches, including arrows to indicate the direction of the VPs.

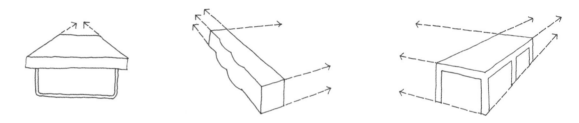

4.

Create detailed drawings of your benches.

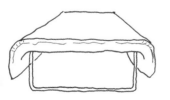
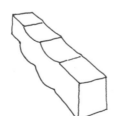

BENCH SPECIFICATIONS from left

Cloud bench
Naoto Fukasawa | 2006

Double Dip bench
Chris Howker | 2006

Florence Knoll bench
Florence Knoll | 1954

29

PLAN, ELEVATION + 3D

This exercise focuses on studying an object in plan, elevation, and perspective. A plan and elevation are important architectural drawings but lack the depth of a three-dimensional (3D) view. However, gaining an understanding of your chair in all dimensions is valuable in appreciating the complexities of three-dimensional form. The chairs in this example were selected for their diversity of forms. Each offers a unique challenge—from fluid curves to a zigzag formation.

1.

Select three chairs While viewing the chairs in three dimensions (real life), imagine and then draw them in plan, as if you were looking straight down at the objects. This view is flat, and not typical of what is seen in real life.

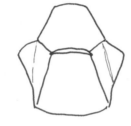

2.

Continuing to view the chairs in three dimensions, imagine and then draw them in elevation, as if you were looking directly from the side. This view is also flat.

3.

Draw the chairs as they are typically viewed, in three dimensions.

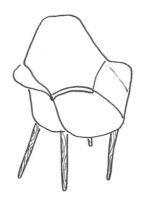

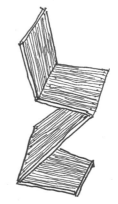

4.

Draw the chairs and show texture and detail. In these examples the legs of the chair on the left are rendered, and the whole of the one on the right, with a wood grain, and a speckled texture is used to evoke the wool fabric on the cushion of the chair in the center. All representation of texture is drawn using the thin pen, which emphasizes the different surfaces without dominating the overall form of the chair.

CHAIR SPECIFICATIONS from left

Organic chair
Charles Eames & Eero Saarinen I 1940

Tulip side chair
Eero Saarinen I 1940

Zig-Zag chair
Gerrit Rietveld I 1934

CIRCLES

It is generally more interesting to provide a three-dimensional or perspective view of an object, interior, or building than a two-dimensional or flat representation, since a three-dimensional view conveys the depth of an object as one would view it in real life. Circular objects are challenging to represent in perspective, since a circle is not viewed as a circle but angled into an oval shape. This exercise gives a method for sketching circles so that they accurately reflect what we see.

1.

Select a round table Set up one horizontal and five vertical guidelines. Using the first vertical guideline, draw your tabletop in plan, which is viewed as a circle (below). Draw three views of the top as you view it in perspective, moving gradually from plan toward elevation. Your fifth and final sketch will be in elevation (below right).

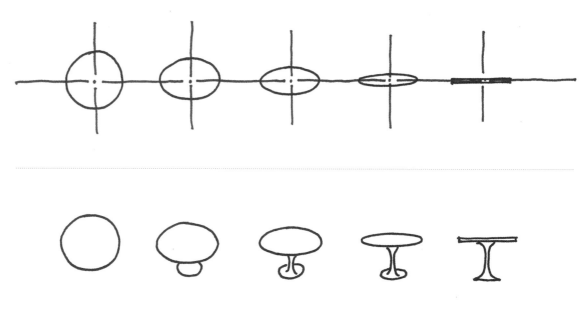

2.

Draw the same five views of the table from plan to elevation, but this time include the base.

3.

Select two more round tables Set up guidelines and practice creating smooth, effortless ovals that are vertically and horizontally symmetrical, then sketch the oval tops of all three tables you have selected, and oval bases if applicable.

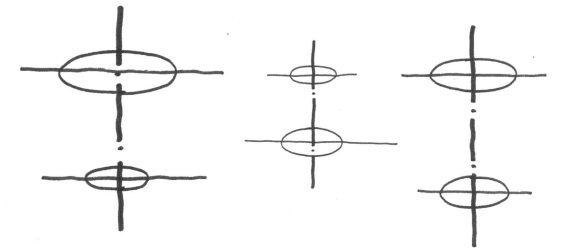

4.

Create line drawings of the three tables with a medium pen.

TABLE SPECIFICATIONS from left

Tulip side table
Eero Saarinen I 1956

Adjustable table E1027
Eileen Gray I 1927

Petal end table
Richard Schultz I 1960

MULTIPLE VIEWPOINTS

In life we move around objects daily, and our point of view changes depending on the way we see our surroundings. It is important to view the same object from many angles and positions. Some objects can be manipulated (such as a desk light) so that one drawing can show many varied viewpoints. This exercise gives the opportunity to study an object in new ways and understand the principles of perspective and foreshortening.

1.

Select three light fixtures: one simple, one complex, and one with a moveable part With your medium pen, sketch the simple light fixture five times. Draw it at different angles and scales to create a balanced composition. It is helpful to create a few thumbnail (small) sketches with various configurations of the fixture to see how the composition reads. These can be very quick, loose outlines of the object with very little detail, just to focus on the overall layout.

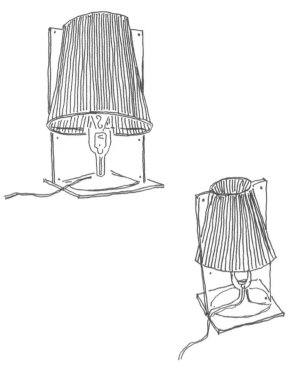

2.

Sketch the complex light fixture with your medium pen from two views; one from below and one from above. As previously stated, line drawings best capture the overall form of the objects; however, any interesting details should be rendered with your thin pen. In this example the lamp has a textured polycarbonate shade; the thin pen was used to draw loose, thin lines that represent the fluted ridges in the plastic shade.

3.

Sketch the light fixture with a moveable part. This lamp has an adjustable arm that moves up and down to redirect the light source. Drawing the arm in multiple positions within one drawing provides a sense of movement.

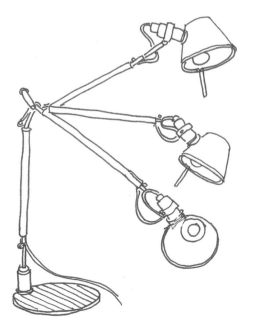

LIGHTING SPECIFICATIONS from left

E27 pendant
Mattias Ståhlbom I 2008

Take lamp
Ferruccio Laviani I 2003

Tolomeo lamp
Michele De Lucchi & Giancarlo Fassina I 1987

APPLIED PATTERN

This exercise explores patterns that are applied, such as in a textile or painted onto the surface. These patterns add character to a sketch, but they can be complex and so it is important to investigate the design before drawing the object.

1.

Select three chairs that incorporate pattern in their design Sketch the pattern on a magnified scale while looking closely at the basic shapes. In this example the patterns include an intricate multicolored floral textile (left), a striped fabric that follows the curve of the ball (center), and a snowflake-inspired design (right).

2.

A black-and-white ink drawing can indicate color through gray values (light/dark contrast). If your pattern has color, use your gray markers to express lightness or darkness. The pattern on the left is multicolored, the pattern in the center is beige and orange, and the pattern on the right is gray and white.

3.

Sketch the chairs with a medium pen, omitting the pattern.

 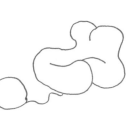 

4.

Draw the chairs with the patterns applied.

5.

Render the patterns with markers to represent light/dark.

CHAIR SPECIFICATIONS from left

Mademoiselle chair
Philippe Starck I 2003

UP5 chair & UP6 ottoman
Gaetano Pesce I 1969

Nanook chair
Philippe Bestenheider I 2008

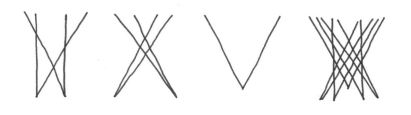

INTEGRATED PATTERN

Decorative patterns can be applied, as in the Applied Pattern exercise (see page 36), but the actual material of the furniture can also form the pattern, as in the steel wire that bends to form the pieces in the examples here.

1.

Select three pieces of furniture with integrated texture. Study the textural elements in your pieces. In these examples, the wire table base is pulled apart and the elements are shown in groups (top row); the wire framework of the chair is shown as individual, overlapping pieces and as an integrated texture (center row); and the wire that forms the base of the second table is exploded (bottom row).

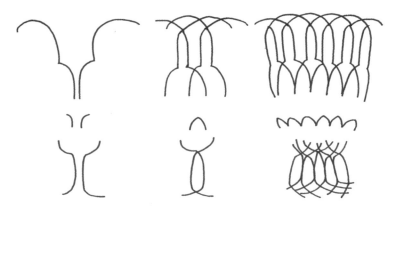

2.

Create a line drawing of each
furniture piece.

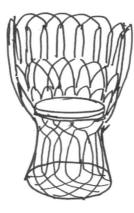

FURNITURE SPECIFICATIONS from top

Cyclone side table
Isamu Noguchi I 1953

Re-trouvé chair
Patricia Urquiola I 2009

Pumpkin side table
Seyhan Özdemir & Sefer Çaglar I 2004

SHADE + SHADOW

Incorporating shade and shadow can create an informative sketch, often with more depth than a simple line drawing. Light creates shadows, patterns, and reflections—elements that add a layer of interest to a drawing. A clear understanding of why and where a shadow occurs is necessary for the drawing to make visual sense, and for the values to add to (not take away from) the drawing. The examples have diverse forms that provide an overall understanding about how shade and shadow affect the appearance of furniture.

1.

Select three chairs Create three thumbnail sketches of your first chair. Select a natural or artificial light source and represent the source direction with a graphic symbol and/or arrow (as shown left). This will give you the opportunity to explore three different directions of light for each chair. Assign the values 1, 2, and 3 to indicate how much light each plane receives; this is the key to creating correct values. Reducing the number of values to three—even if there are many more in reality—emphasizes the three-dimensional aspect of an object. The side facing the light source will be the brightest, since it is the one getting the largest amount of light. That side has value 1 (bright). The side adjoining the brightest has value 2 (medium), and the side farthest from the brightest side has value 3 (dark). On your three thumbnail sketches, indicate the values that occur on each plane of the chair as a result of your light source, labeling 1, 2, or 3 to indicate the shading intensity. Repeat this exercise for the other two chairs selected.

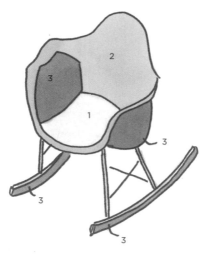

2.

Select one thumbnail for each chair to create a more detailed sketch. Render the three light values with your 10 percent, 30 percent, and 50 percent markers, or use the 10 percent, 50 percent, and 90 percent markers for more contrast.

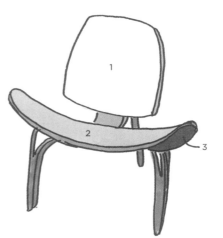

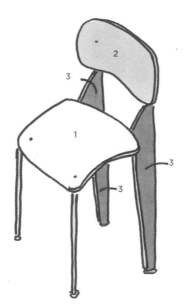

3.

Using the sun or a tall floor or ceiling lamp, cast the light source on each chair. When the light hits the object, not only will this create different light values on the surface of the object but a shadow will appear on the ground plane below the object. If the sun (or artificial light source) hits the right side of the object, a shadow will occur on the left side of the object on the ground surface. Draw the object and shadow as it appears. Without an actual light source, it is difficult to predict the shape of the shadows that will be cast, especially with unusual chair forms. However, with practice you will become more familiar with the way objects cast shadows, especially in the case of simpler forms. Repeat this exercise with light from a different direction, so that you have cast two shadows for each chair.

4.

Select another view for each chair and create a drawing that combines all of the exercises discussed. Sketch and render each chair with a distinct light source, including the cast shadow that results on the ground plane, to create a drawing that expresses line, form, light, shade/shadow, depth, and three-dimensionality.

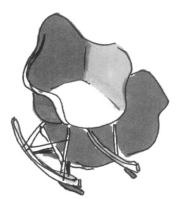

CHAIR SPECIFICATIONS from left

Eames molded plastic armchair rocker (RAR)
Charles & Ray Eames I 1948

Standard SP chair
Jean Prouvé I 1930

Shell chair
Hans Wegner I 1963

COMPOSITION

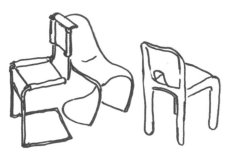

Until now, all of the exercises have focused on a single object. In reality, we view many objects at a time, and these overlapping, complex arrangements can lead to dynamic sketches. This will be most evident as we draw interior space—where furniture, lighting, and architectural elements are integrated into a single view. This exercise builds on the previous exercises to create a composition of three chairs, first with a line drawing and then using the principles of shade and shadow to complete the drawing.

1.

Select three groups of three chairs
Create thumbnail layouts to find the best arrangement for your group of three chairs. Turn each chair to a different, interesting angle and overlap them slightly so that they interact with each other. An odd number of chairs (three or five) works best to create a balanced composition. Draw each group of three chairs, using the thick pen to emphasize the form.

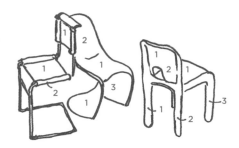

2.

Indicate the light source for your composition, and label the chairs 1, 2, or 3 to indicate the light values.

3.

Draw the composition and use markers
to render the chairs according to the
light values. Cast the shadows on
the ground plane and render with
a dark marker (such as 80 percent or
90 percent).

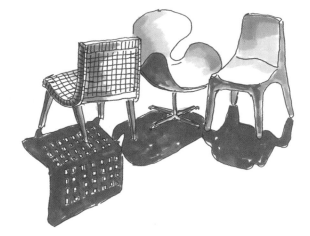

CHAIR SPECIFICATIONS

left

Model No. S33 chair
Mart Stam I 1926

Panton chair
Verner Panton I 1959

Universale chair
Joe Colombo I 1965

center

Eames molded plastic chair
Charles & Ray Eames I 1950

Military chair
Gerrit Rietveld I 1923

Ant chair
Arne Jacobsen I 1951

right

No. 654 W chair
Jens Risom I 1941

Swan chair
Arne Jacobsen I 1957

Bofinger Chair
Helmut Bätzner I 1964

2.
INTERIORS

ONE-POINT PERSPECTIVE

A one-point perspective drawing is a three-dimensional view of a space from the location of the viewer (you) and represented in two-dimensional form on paper. A technical perspective drawing uses a series of steps to draft a three-dimensional grid of a space that includes the floor, walls, and ceiling—allowing one to plot furniture, columns, and other interior elements within this defined grid. The concept of this book is to draw what you see; therefore, a grid is not necessary. A careful study of your view and an understanding of the principles of perspective will be enough to create well-proportioned spaces that are accurate and to scale. The following process will give you a deeper understanding of the interior architecture and three-dimensional qualities of a space while demonstrating how to sketch a one-point perspective view.

The five principles of one-point perspective:

1. All horizontal lines are parallel to the horizon line.
2. All vertical lines are parallel (and perpendicular to the horizon line).
3. All diagonal lines recede to the VP; these are referred to as orthogonal lines.
4. All objects get smaller as they recede into the distance.
5. All objects along orthogonal lines become foreshortened (meaning the dimension of these objects will be shorter than the dimensions of objects not on the orthogonal lines).

As discussed in the Perspective Basics exercise (see page 28), a one-point perspective is the simplest view in that all of the elements on the orthogonal lines recede to one VP. In interiors, this occurs when you are directly facing an elevation or wall.

1.

Select an interior space and position yourself facing a wall Sketch the back wall of your view in elevation; label the floor and ceiling planes. This is the wall that will form the framework for your one-point perspective.

ceiling

floor

2.

Identify your sightline on the drawing, also called the horizon line. This line is typically 5 feet off the floor, which is considered average standing eye level. If you are drawing the interior from a seated view, the sightline is typically 3 feet off the floor, which is considered average seated eye level. Depending on your ceiling height, you can estimate where the 5-foot horizon line would fall. If you have a low ceiling height, such as 7 or 8 feet, the sight line will be closer to the ceiling than if you are drawing a space with a high ceiling.

horizon

3.

Locate and indicate your VP on the horizon line. This is determined from the location where you are standing in the space and is considered to be the most remote distance able to be viewed by the eye. For example, if you are standing in the exact center of the room, the VP will be centered on the horizon line within the room; if you standing left of the center, it should be drawn as such. Views left or right of center, even just 1 foot from the centerline, are often more realistic, as we don't usually enter or view an interior at the exact center of the room. You can draw many views of your space by moving the VP along the horizon line each time you sketch, creating different points of view.

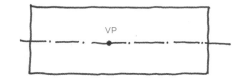

4.

Draw four dashed lines, each starting at your VP and extending to the four corners of your wall.

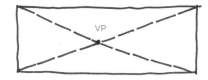

5.

Extend the lines from each corner to create your floor, side walls, and ceiling in three dimensions—as they protrude toward the viewer (you).

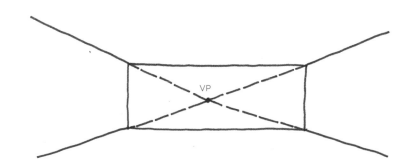

6.

Draw the floor, side walls, and ceiling without guidelines; you have now constructed a three-dimensional view of your space. Indicate the VP, as you will use this point to construct the interior space.

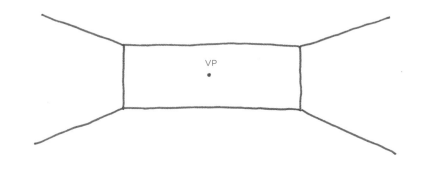

7.

Within this framework, draw the details of the interior architecture—referred to as non-moving elements. All of the elements that fall along the diagonal lines, referred to as orthogonal lines, will recede back to the VP. Using dashed guidelines to represent the orthogonal lines that radiate out from your VP is helpful in drawing these elements with accuracy. Keep in mind that all horizontal lines are parallel to the horizon line, and all vertical lines are perpendicular to the horizon line.

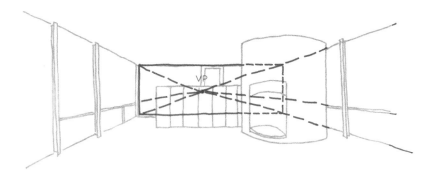

8.

Draw the interior architecture without guidelines.

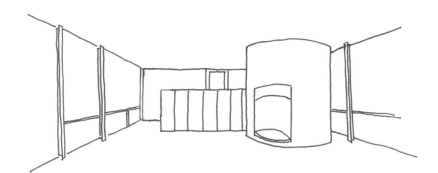

9.

Using the same perspective principles, draw the decorative elements in your space, such as furniture, lighting, artwork, rugs, etc.; these are referred to as moving elements. The use of dashed guidelines that radiate out from your VP will ensure that all of your elements on the diagonal recede back to this point.

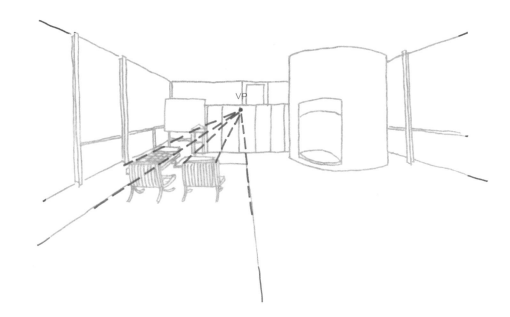

10.

Draw the interior in its entirety, without guidelines, including all architectural and decorative elements.

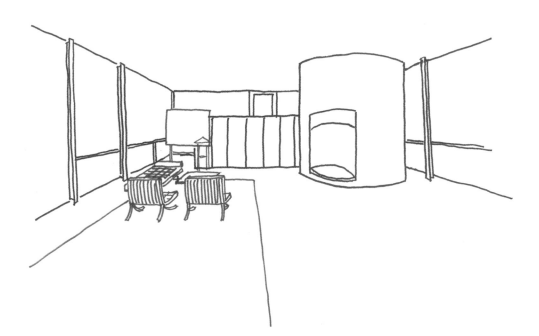

INTERIOR SPECIFICATION

Glass House
Philip Johnson I New Canaan, Connecticut, USA I 1949

TWO-POINT PERSPECTIVE

The main difference between a one-point and a two-point perspective (as the name suggests) is that there are two VPs instead of one. This was touched upon in the Perspective Basics exercise (see page 28), but will now be explored in greater depth and applied to interior space. A two-point perspective occurs when the viewer sees a space from an angle, such as looking into the corner of a room. The floor, wall, and ceiling on one side of the corner will recede to VP1, and the floor, wall, and ceiling on the other side of the corner will recede to VP2. As you practise drawing two-point perspectives, you will start to understand which elements recede toward VP1 and which elements recede toward VP2.

The five principles of two-point perspective:

1. The only horizontal line is the horizon line.
2. All vertical lines are parallel (and perpendicular to the horizon line).
3. All diagonal lines recede to either VP1 or VP2; these are referred to as orthogonal lines.
4. All objects get smaller as they recede into the distance.
5. All objects along the orthogonal lines become foreshortened.

1.

Select a view looking into a corner
Sketch the corner line where the two walls meet, and locate your floor and ceiling planes.

2.

Draw your horizon line at 5 feet above your floor line.

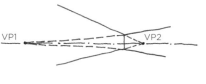

3.

Use dashed lines to extend the floor and ceiling lines from where the corner meets the floor and where the corner meets the ceiling to find the two VPs. This is a freehand drawing, not a technical drawing—you are representing what you see and using the principles of perspective as a guide. Therefore, you can tweak the angles of your floor and ceiling so that your VPs fall on the horizon line, or modify any elements of your sketch so that it works for your drawing.

4.

Draw the framework for your space indicating the locations of the VPs.

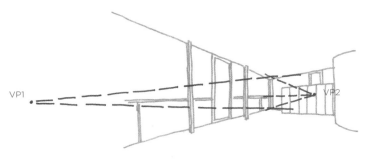

VP1 • - - - - - - - - - - - - - - - - - VP2

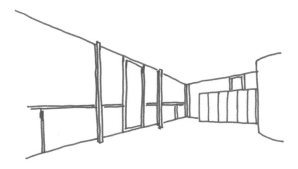

5.

Use your VPs to radiate dashed orthogonal lines that will serve as guides to draw the interior architecture.

6.

Draw the interior architecture without the guidelines.

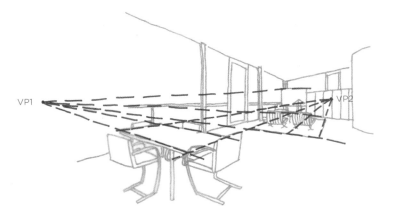

VP1 ◄ - - - - - - - - - - - - - - - - ► VP2

7.

Use your VPs and orthogonal lines to draw the decorative elements within your space.

8.

Draw your two-point perspective view in totality, with architectural and decorative detail.

INTERIOR SPECIFICATION

Glass House
Philip Johnson I New Canaan, Connecticut, USA I 1949

ONE-POINT ABSTRACTION

Now that you have completed the one- and two-point perspective exercises, this one will continue to build upon your framework of knowledge, using abstraction as a sketching tool to examine perspective. Studying the triangular shapes that radiate out from a VP will give you an understanding of how elements are viewed in perspective. It emphasizes the principles that objects decrease in size as they recede into the distance and that all of the elements along the orthogonal lines within a view will reach the same VP. Applying these concepts within an abstract framework reinforces the ideas behind the representation of three-dimensional interiors.

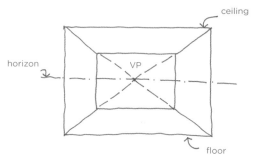

1.

Select a space viewed from a one-point perspective

Set up your interior framework as discussed in the One-Point Perspective exercise (see page 50); sketch the back wall, note the horizon line, locate the VP in your space, and indicate the floor and ceiling planes.

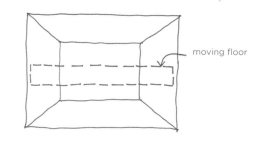

2.

Use dashes for the significant architectural elements within your view. In the example there is a "moving floor," which can be raised and lowered to align with the fixed floors of the house. This element is indicated with a dashed line.

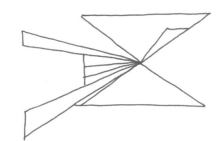

3.

Study your view closely, focusing on and sketching the triangular shapes that protrude toward the viewer from the VP.

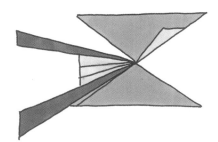

4.

Render the triangles with your markers using darker values to represent the triangular shapes that protrude closer toward the viewer and lighter values for the triangular shapes that are farther from the viewer.

5.

Sketch the interior elements that you
defined with the triangular shapes.

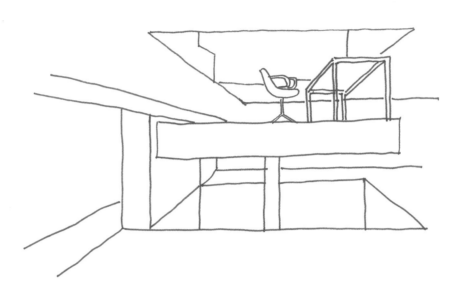

6.

Complete your drawing, incorporating
architectural and decorative detail. In this
example the addition of stairs, books,
and modern artwork creates a narrative
that gives the space context and depth.

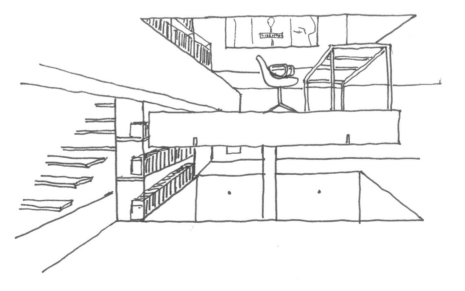

INTERIOR SPECIFICATION

Maison Bordeaux
Rem Koolhaas I Bordeaux, France I 1998

TWO-POINT ABSTRACTION

This exercise uses the same method as the One-Point Abstraction exercise (see page 56) but incorporates a two-point perspective to create triangular abstractions. Since there are two VPs, there will be two groups of triangles—one group that extends from VP1 and one group that extends from VP2. These two groups can also be combined to create a layered study of triangles from both VPs. This will help you to understand which objects recede to which VP.

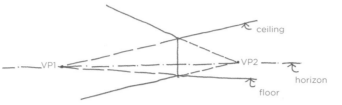

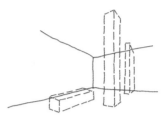

1.
Select a space viewed from a two-point perspective Follow the steps from the Two-Point Perspective exercise (see page 54) to create a framework of your two-point perspective view. Draw the back corner, floor, and ceiling lines, locate the horizon line, and identify the two VPs.

2.
Use dashes for the significant interior architectural elements within your framework. In this example structural columns and a large display unit define the interior space.

3.
Sketch the triangular shapes that protrude from VP1.

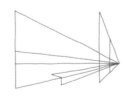

4.
Render the triangles with your markers using darker values to represent the triangular shapes that protrude closer toward the viewer and lighter values for the triangular shapes that are farther from the viewer.

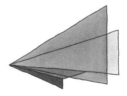

5.
Sketch the triangular shapes that protrude from VP2.

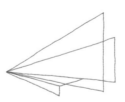

6.
Render the triangles, again using darker values for the triangular shapes closer to the viewer.

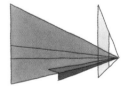

7.

Sketch both sets of triangular shapes—those that radiate from VP1 and those that radiate from VP2.

8.

Render the shapes so that the triangular shapes coming from VP1 are dark (80 percent) and those coming from VP2 are light (20 percent).

9.

Render the shapes so that the triangular shapes coming from VP1 are light (20 percent) and those coming from VP2 are dark (80 percent).

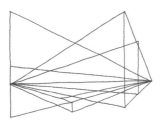

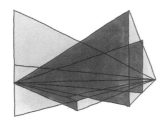

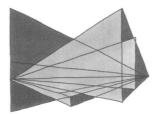

10.

Sketch the basic interior elements that you defined with the triangular shapes.

11.

Complete your drawing, adding informative details to give the viewer a sense of being in the space. This example includes architectural elements such as lighting, and decorative elements such as clothing rails and mannequins, to show the function of a retail store.

INTERIOR SPECIFICATION

Calvin Klein Collection Store
John Pawson I New York, USA I 1995

TRANSITIONAL SPACE

This exercise studies transitional spaces—spaces that connect the exterior to the interior, or link two interior spaces. Although often overshadowed by formal areas, transitional spaces can be very interesting to sketch as they reflect a person's experience upon entering an interior. In this example the upper level of the building protrudes over a public walkway to create a modernist porch; oval glass cutouts in the ground give views to a display below the walkway. The following series of diagrammatical studies help to define this transitional space.

1.

Select a transitional space that leads into an interior Draw the vertical planes that create the boundaries of your transitional space.

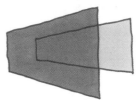

2.

Using markers, render these imaginary planes; in darker gray for the plane that is closer to the viewer and lighter gray for the plane that is farther from the viewer.

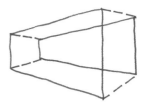

3.

Draw the vertical planes and use dashed lines to connect the planes visually, creating a room with boundaries (e.g. a floor, ceiling, and two walls).

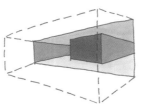

4.

Use dashes for the transitional space, while using a solid line to draw the formal interior into which it leads. Abstract the architectural elements of the interior and render them with your markers (elements closer to the viewer darker, elements farther from the viewer lighter).

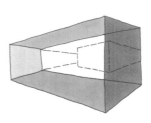

5.

Complete a sketch that is the inverse of the previous step: draw your transitional space with a solid line and dash in the elements of the formal interior. Use your markers to render the transitional spaces. Again, elements closer to the viewer are darker, while elements farther from the viewer are lighter.

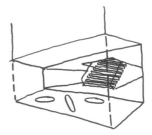

6.

Create a drawing of the transitional space and the interior using your thick pen, and add detail of significant elements (in this example, the wide stairway in the center of the interior and the glass cutouts in the ground). Use dashed lines to create the imaginary boundaries of the transitional space.

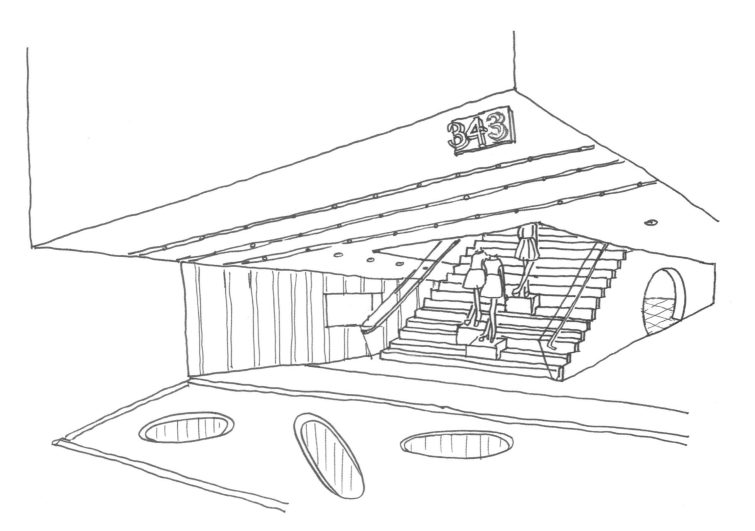

7.

Draw the transitional space and the interior in detail. Here, the addition of retail products and mannequins shows the function of the space; floor cutouts and wall finishes show design detail; and signage ties the space to its urban context.

INTERIOR SPECIFICATION

Prada Epicenter

Rem Koolhaas I Los Angeles, USA I 2004

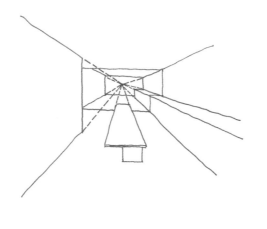

INTERIOR + EXTERIOR

This exercise explores the contrast between being in an interior space looking out onto an exterior space and being on the exterior looking back into the interior. When inside a space, the interior elements are dominant; however, incorporating an exterior view in an interior view can create a more richly layered space than if the view ended at the exterior wall. Differentiating between interior and exterior space is another way to understand the layering of perspective and continues to build on the principles previously explored.

1.

Select an interior/exterior space separated by glass As in previous examples, the first step is to study your view and set up your perspective framework. Here a one-point perspective is used. Draw the back wall of the interior space, indicate your horizon line, locate your VP, use dashes to draw the guidelines that radiate from the VP to the corners of the wall, and draw the solid lines that form the floor, ceiling, and walls of your room. In this example a counter on the right continues from the interior through a glass wall into the exterior, blurring the boundary between interior and exterior.

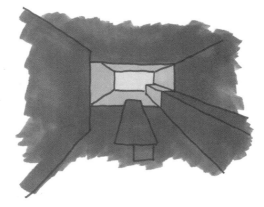

2.

Use your markers to emphasize the elements of the interior compared with the exterior. Since objects closer to the viewer are darker, while objects lighten as the distance increases, render your elements from dark to light as they recede to the exterior.

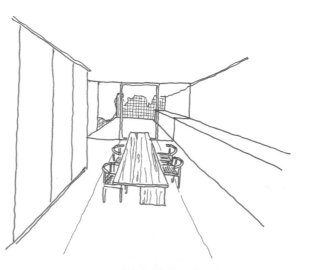

3.

Draw the space in more detail, adding architectural and decorative elements, as well as the view through the glass to the exterior.

4.

Repeat steps 1 and 2, but this time switch the view so that you are looking from the exterior into the interior. In this example the counter is now seen on the left as it continues from the exterior through the glass into the interior.

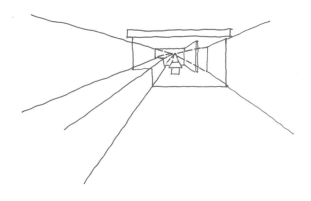

5.

Use the darkest values to render elements closer to the viewer and lighter values for those elements farther from the viewer.

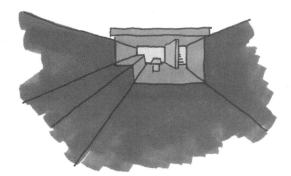

6.

Draw in detail both the exterior space and the interior space as seen through the glass.

INTERIOR SPECIFICATION

Pawson House
John Pawson I London, UK I 1994

WINDOW FRAMES

The previous exercises studied transitional spaces and interior/exterior boundaries. This one focuses on the detail of a window or glass wall that separates inside from outside. Whether a simple window or a complex wall of glass, interesting patterns and shadows are created by the position and depth of the glass within the wall, or the structural or decorative elements within the window. Emphasizing the three-dimensional aspect of the window adds another layer to an interior view that looks out onto an exterior.

1.

Select an interior with exterior glass window/wall Create a dashed grid to lay out the architectural system of your glass window/wall. Use your thick pen to abstract the gridded system.

2.

Draw the wall/window layout. In this example the building's quilted glass exterior has diamond-shaped windows set into a diagonal grid.

3.

As you approach your window/wall from different directions, you will see the depth of the structure/frame. Use arrows to indicate the direction from which you are approaching the window (e.g. from above, from below, from the left, or from the right).

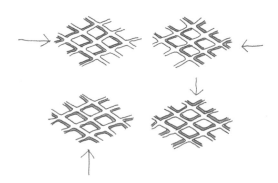

4.

Render the thickness of the wall/window frame with your markers.

5.

Select one of the viewing angles and use this to represent your interior and the depth that results from the wall thickness. Render the thickness with your marker. Using your thin pen (so as not to overshadow your interior), draw the exterior context, such as buildings and vegetation, as viewed through the window.

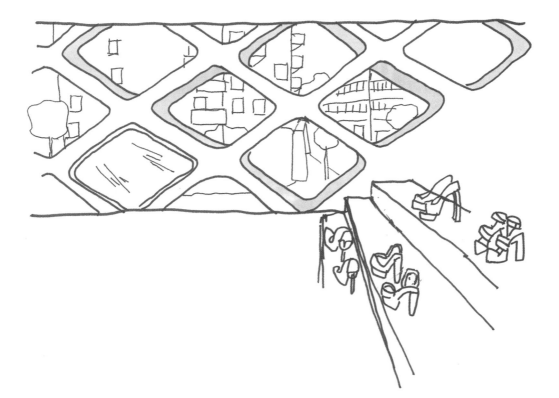

INTERIOR SPECIFICATION

Prada Aoyama

Herzog & de Meuron I Tokyo, Japan I 2003

REPETITION

When drawing a group of repetitive objects, it is effective to set up perspective guidelines and to study the forms as they recede to the VP. Instead of laying out the interior architectural framework first, in this exercise you draw the objects in perspective, and then add the overall interior architecture of the space. Normally, you would start large (the interior) and then add the smaller elements (the furniture), but complex decorative groupings can also be explored initially as a study, and then incorporated into your space—as in this exercise. Part 1 explores a single repeating element; Part 2 moves on to examine a group of repeating elements.

1.

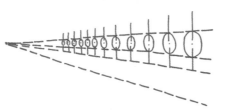

Part 1: Select a view of a single repeating element Use dashed guidelines to block out your objects as they recede toward the VP. In this example four guidelines recede to the VP, each outlining the same part of the bar stools set in a row (top of back, bottom of back, seat height, and where the back legs meet the floor). Set up vertical guidelines at the centerlines of your objects. Since objects decrease in size as they recede to the VP, the spacing between your guidelines should gradually decrease the closer they get to the VP. Draw one part of your object on the centerlines (in this case, the oval backs of the bar stools are seen decreasing in size as they move away from the viewer).

2.

Sketch the abstracted forms of your objects, as seen decreasing in scale the closer they get to the VP. Use your markers to define the shapes that occur, much as you did in the Abstraction exercises (see pages 56–59).

3.

Draw the objects in detail and add the interior architectural context.

INTERIOR SPECIFICATION

Sanderson Hotel
Philippe Starck I London, UK I 2000

4.

Part 2: Select a view of a group of repeating elements When sketching a group of repeating objects, it is helpful to break up the group into separate studies. In this example the furniture is one element of the group, and the carpet and wall decoration make up another element. They are studied and sketched separately and then drawn together in the final sketch, which also incorporates the interior architecture. Again, use dashed guidelines to block out your objects as they recede toward the VP. Here, guidelines are used to define the tops of the banquettes, the tables, and where the back legs of the chairs meet the floor; vertical centerlines indicate the locations of the tables.

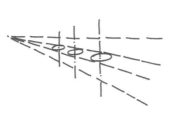

7.

Render this group of objects.

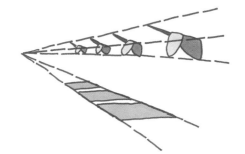

5.

Sketch the abstracted forms of your objects and use your markers to define the shapes that occur.

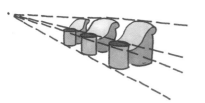

6.

Repeat the same steps with your other sub-group of objects.

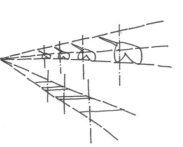

8.

Draw the two sub-groups of furniture together and add the interior architectural context.

INTERIOR SPECIFICATION
....
Faena Hotel
Philippe Starck I Buenos Aires, Argentina I 2006

CONTINUOUS LINE

In keeping with the principle that the process of sketching matters more than what the final sketch looks like, this exercise underlines the importance of intense study of an interior both before and during a sketch. After studying the interior, decide where to put down your pen point, as you will lift it off the paper only once or not at all until the entire interior is sketched. This will help you to practice your line consistency, since constant lifting of the pen off the paper can result in a scratchy line, while a confident, even line enhances the drawing and emphasizes the subject.

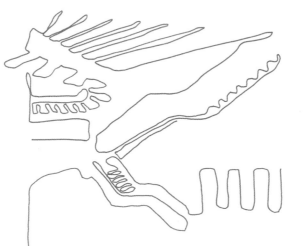

1.

Select an interior The idea is to study your interior carefully and practice drawing with a smooth, fluid consistent line. This example was completed with two lines. Move your pen slowly, taking in the interior elements and drawing over existing lines if necessary.

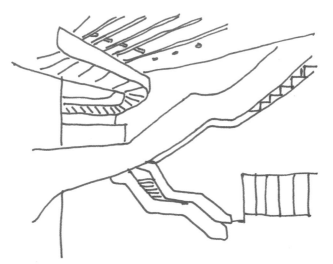

2.

Draw your interior view, taking your pen off the paper as needed. However, the less often your pen comes off the paper, the more fluid your line will appear.

3.

Select a second view of the same interior Draw the interior with one pen line. Do not take your pen off the paper until you have completed the sketch. Your line may zigzag through the space in order to keep it on the paper, as in this example where diagonal lines connect the free-floating strip lights.

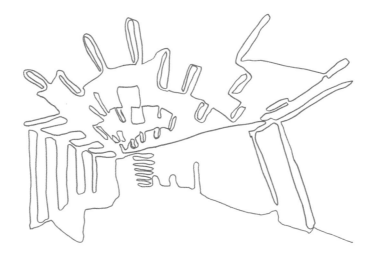

4.

Draw your interior view, taking your pen off the paper as needed.

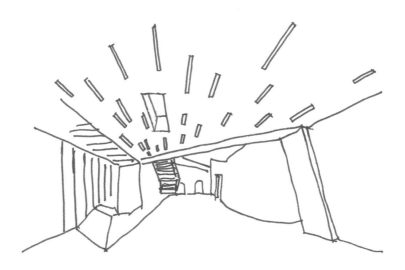

INTERIOR SPECIFICATION

MAXXI: Museum of XXI Century Arts
Zaha Hadid I Rome, Italy I 2003

SCULPTURAL STUDY

1.

Part 1: Select a sculptural staircase Look closely at your stair and create a loose outline of the room to anchor it. Place your pen at the edge of your outline, and begin to sketch the stair without looking at the paper. Repeat this two more times.

This exercise emphasizes the sculptural aspects of an interior architectural element such as a curved stair or ceiling. It involves making a sketch while looking at the sculptural element, not the paper, at all times. This reinforces the study of the subject, with less emphasis on the sketch itself. Not surprisingly, many sketches done without looking at the paper have a loose, carefree quality that is ideal when sketching sculptural elements.

2.

Look at the paper as needed to sketch the space in its totality, including interior details (such as the chairs on display in this example). Use the perspective tools you have learned.

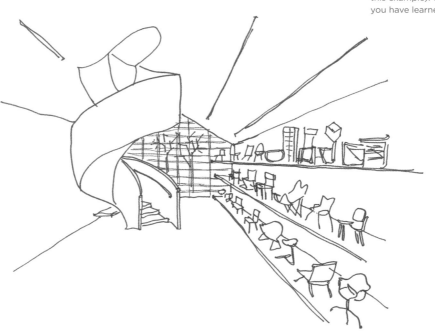

INTERIOR SPECIFICATION

VitraHaus
Herzog & de Meuron I Weil am Rhein, Germany I 2010

3.

Part 2: Select a sculptural ceiling Draw an outline of where the ceiling meets the wall. Place your pen at the edge of your outline, and begin to sketch the ceiling while not looking at your paper. Repeat this two more times. In this example a tangled web of lines is actually a complex grid of glass panes that connects the buildings along the perimeter and inside of an interior courtyard.

4.

Sketch the space in its totality, again, looking at the paper as needed.

INTERIOR SPECIFICATION

Great Court at the British Museum
Foster + Partners I London, UK I 2000

PEOPLE

The best way to show scale in a sketch of an interior (or exterior) view is to add a human figure or figures. Without doing so, it is difficult for the viewer to discern the size of the architectural elements. Including human figures also shows how people interact with the space (e.g. sitting in a restaurant or walking through a museum). It indicates how the space is actually used—creating a lively and energetic sketch.

1.

Practice drawing a variety of human figures. These can be outlines of people doing different activities—walking, standing, or sitting. Figures drawn with little detail, as seen in the example left, provide the needed scale but do not distract from the interior or architecture of the space. There are many stylistic approaches, from abstract to realistic. You need to find what works with your drawing style and the feeling you want to convey in your sketches.

2.

In perspective sketches the eye level of all average adult figures on the same ground plane will align. People who are closer to the viewer are larger, and people who are farther away are smaller, but their eye level remains the same. Use your thick pen to draw a dashed horizontal line indicating the eye level, then draw figures at different proximities to the viewer.

3.

Select an interior that includes people
Draw your interior using the tools
discussed previously in this chapter
(guidelines, perspectives, etc.). In this
example a multi-height atrium space
consists of overlapping levels and
bridges, and people are seen at many
different heights. In a view with one level,
there will be one eye level, and all the
figures' eyes will line up along the
imaginary guideline. If a view has more
than one level, as in this example, there
will be a corresponding number of
imaginary guidelines. On the first level,
the eye level of all the figures is at the
same height, although the figures
themselves are larger (closer) and
smaller (farther away). On the second
level, people are seen standing against
the handrail and share the same eye level.

INTERIOR SPECIFICATION
....
East Building at the National Gallery of Art
I. M. Pei I Washington, DC, USA I 1978

Select an interior with three interesting views Sketch the element in your space that recedes into the background. In this example a low wall spirals up and around through the space. Repeat this exercise for two other views in the space.

VIEWPOINTS

Three-dimensional objects and spaces can comprise complex layers; some elements protrude while others recede. This principle was first discussed in Furniture + Lighting and it applies equally to interiors, albeit at a larger scale. This exercise studies an element of a space that moves away from the viewer. Examining the parts of an element that are closer to and farther away from the viewer reinforces the concept of layering—and how we view objects in three dimensions. This exercise also emphasizes the principle that objects are darker when closer to the viewer and lighter as they recede into the distance.

2.

For each of your views, render the elements from dark (closer to the viewer) to light (as it recedes away from the viewer).

3.

Draw the space with detail incorporating the studied element. This example includes details such as artwork and lighting to show the function of the museum. It also incorporates people, which expresses scale and animates the interior.

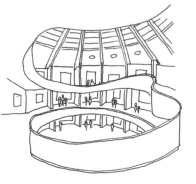

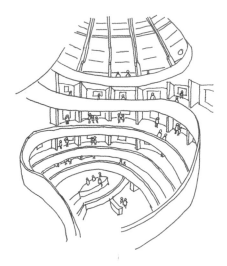

INTERIOR SPECIFICATION

Solomon R. Guggenheim Museum
Frank Lloyd Wright I New York, USA I 1959

FOREGROUND + BACKGROUND

To draw interior spaces well, you need to understand the principles of layering. Complex interiors incorporate layers that progress from foreground to background (front to back). This exercise studies these layers and uses varied intensities of gray to communicate depth. This may be necessary when a line drawing reads very flat or is difficult to understand because of a lack of information. Adding gray values can help to communicate what elements recede and what elements protrude. This is not a shading exercise; the values do not derive from a light source. It is a study to further explore elements as they recede into the distance. After completing the exercise, you can judge which rendered sketch indicates depth most effectively.

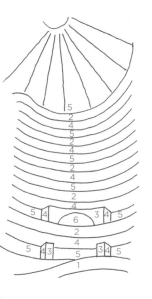

1.

Select an interior with complex layers
Sketch the interior and use numbers to indicate which elements are closer or farther away from the viewer, beginning with 1 for the closest. In this example the layers (low wall, ceiling, and back wall) make a line drawing difficult to understand.

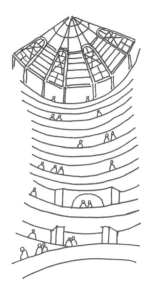

2.

Draw your interior in greater detail and include people to show scale.

3.

Use markers to render your sketch, using the darker gray for the closest element (1). As the numbers increase, the gray value will decrease. While it was difficult to perceive depth in the line drawing, this rendered version reveals the three-dimensionality of the space and shows the importance of value in certain sketches.

4.

Repeat the previous step, but this time render your sketch using the lighter gray for the closest element (1). As the numbers increase, the gray value will increase.

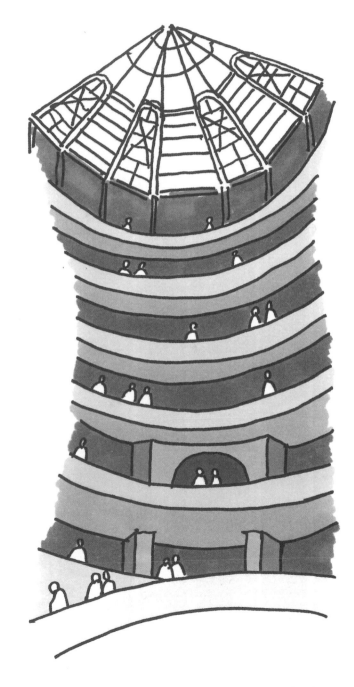

INTERIOR SPECIFICATION

Solomon R. Guggenheim Museum
Frank Lloyd Wright | New York, USA | 1959

1.

Select an interior Create a thumbnail layout of your view. Add a box around the view, and label it as 1. Draw a second, smaller box using a large-dashed line around an architectural element you wish to magnify, and label this as 2. Finally, draw a third, even smaller box, using a short-dashed line around an aspect of this element that requires closer scrutiny.

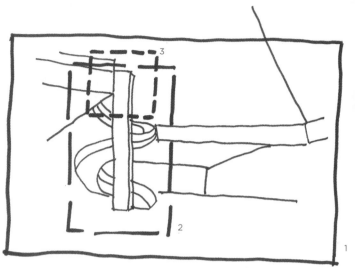

MAGNIFICATION

Interiors can be complex. An overall sketch does not always clearly convey the detail or uniqueness of a space. This exercise uses magnification to move the viewer closer into a space for a sharper view. First you will sketch an interior space, then zoom in to a particular architectural element, and then zoom in even closer to sketch a detail of this element.

2.

Draw the interior view in box 1. This line drawing captures the significant elements within the overall space.

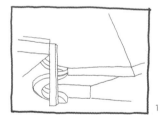

3.

Add more detail to your drawing.

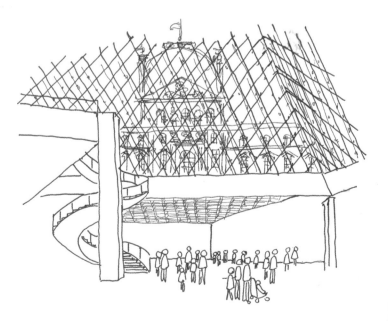

4.

Draw the architectural element in box 2.

5.

Add more detail to your drawing.

2

6.

Draw the detail of the architectural element in box 3.

7.

Add more detail to your drawing.

3

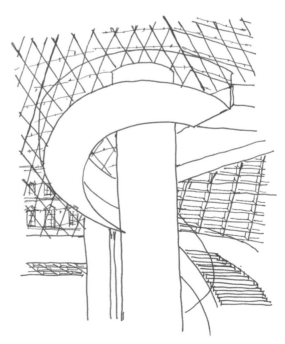

INTERIOR SPECIFICATION

Louvre Pyramid
I. M. Pei I Paris, France I 1989

INTERIOR SHADING

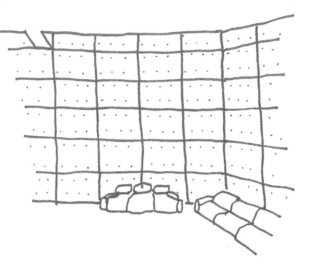

1.

Part 1: Select a simple interior space that receives sunlight Study your interior space and create a line drawing using the principles you have learned. In this example there is a slit of light where the back wall meets the ceiling—creating very strong shadows that are cast off a structural beam.

In the Furniture + Lighting section, you learned to shade a single piece or group of furniture by indicating the direction of the light source, giving values to the subject using varied intensities of gray to render the values, and rendering the shadow cast on the floor with the darkest gray. Although the scale of an interior space is much larger than that of a chair or group of chairs, the same principles apply. It is more difficult to alter natural light (although possible with window treatments) than it is using the artificial light of a lamp, which can be easily adjusted to get an interesting shadow. If you plan to use natural light, you will need to visit an interior at different times of the day to see how the natural movement of the sun in the sky changes the shadows within the space. This example uses natural light.

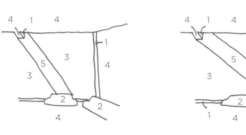

2.

Create three thumbnail sketches of your space at three different times of the day. Observe and record the shadows that result. Assign values for the shading, starting at 1 for the lightest value and rising to 5 for the darkest value.

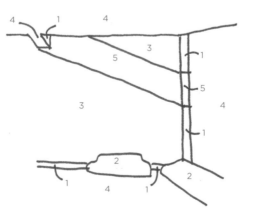

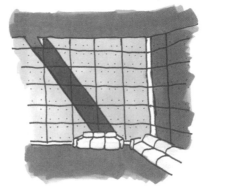
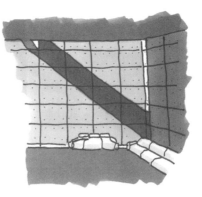

3.

Render each sketch to represent the interior light patterns and shadows that occur throughout the day. For simplicity, restrict the lighting values to a maximum of five, and do not render the areas with value 1 (i.e. leave the white of the paper). Then use 20 percent for value 2, 40 percent for value 3, 60 percent for value 4, and 80 percent for value 5. Avoid using 100 percent—pure black dominates the sketch and detracts from the shadowy quality of the gray values.

INTERIOR SPECIFICATION

Koshino House
Tadao Ando I Ashiya, Hyogo, Japan I 1984

4.

**Part 2: Select a complex interior space
that receives sunlight** Block out the
architectural elements of your space and
create a map of shadow intensities by
numbering areas from 1 (lightest) to
5 (darkest). Restrict your values to a
maximum of five, no matter how complex
your view, so you can create contrast
with your markers (remember you have
only five gray values if you start at
10 percent and use odd percentages
for more contrast, e.g. 30 percent,
50 percent, 70 percent, and 90 percent).
In this example there is a narrow slit cut
into the back wall behind the altar,
forming a cross that radiates natural
sunlight and creates interesting light
patterns and gradations of shadow.

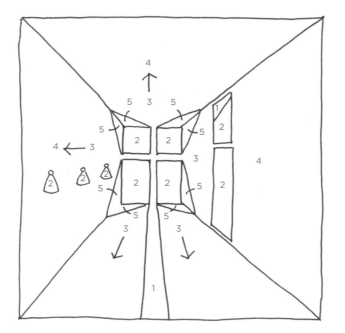

5.

Create a line drawing of the interior
architecture. In this example the joints
in the concrete walls and ceiling create
a grid, which helps to frame the space.

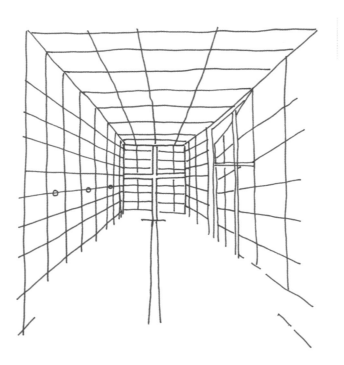

6.

Add furniture and lighting to the space. Use your knowledge of perspective to locate your horizon line and VP so that all the architectural elements and furniture recede to a common point.

7.

Use your markers to block out the shading in your space according to your diagram. For ultimate contrast, and to emphasize the brightness of the lightest value, do not render the brightest spaces—those noted as 1 on the diagram. Just leave the white of the paper. Use 20 percent for value 2, 30 percent for value 3, 40 percent for value 4, and 50 percent for value 5.

8.

Add another layer of gray to your drawing. Use 20 percent for value 2, 40 percent for value 3, 60 percent for value 4, and 80 percent for value 5. If you really want your dark to "pop," use 90 percent for value 5. More contrast will create a more dynamic and dramatic interior sketch. After completing the two versions of this view, you can decide if you prefer a more diluted or contrasted rendering for your space.

INTERIOR SPECIFICATION

Church of the Light
Tadao Ando I Osaka, Japan I 1989

3.
ARCHITECTURE

SYMMETRY + PATTERN

Symmetry in buildings is more difficult to draw than it appears. It is a challenge to mirror the proportions and details of one side of a building. This exercise uses a centerline as a guide to draw a symmetrical building. Then, it explores what happens when you repeat this mirroring process multiple times to create interesting patterns which make you look at the building in a new way. The building in this example has a simple outline but incorporates many striking patterns within its symmetry.

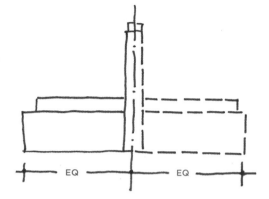

1.

Select a symmetrical building Use dashes to draw the centerline and block out the basic elements of one side of your building. Use a dimension line to mark the spacing on either side of the centerline as equal. With a dashed line, mirror the building on the opposite side of the centerline. You will need to look closely at your building and your sketch. It is essential to keep the basic forms of your building accurately in proportion.

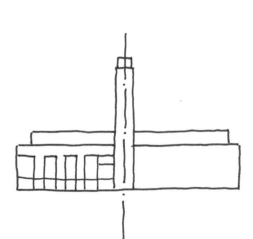

2.

On one side of your sketch, add the basic building detail, such as the outline of the windows and other architectural elements. You will mirror these elements on the opposite side of your centerline in later steps.

3.

Sketch your building again, this time without the detail, and draw a horizontal guideline at the ground level of your building. Using the approach described in the Mirror Image exercise (see page 22), mirror your entire building below the guideline.

4.

Add the basic architectural elements that you sketched on one side of your building.

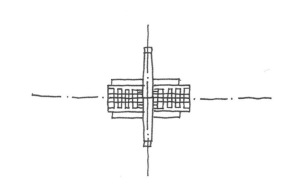

5.

Set up a vertical guideline at one end of your building pair and a horizontal guideline at the bottom edge of your building pair. Mirror the pair vertically and then horizontally so that you have a sketch of eight buildings.

6.

Render the buildings to emphasize verticality by using darker values for the vertical elements.

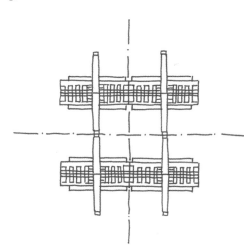

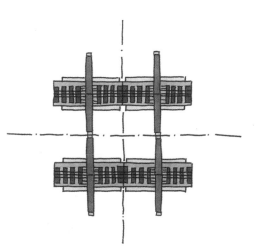

7.

Render the buildings to emphasize horizontality by using darker values for the horizontal elements.

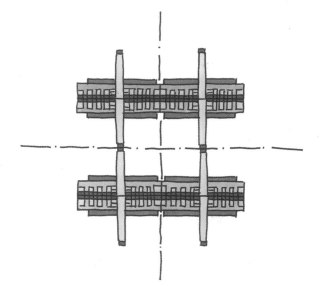

8.

Mirror your cluster of eight buildings vertically and then horizontally to create a basic outline of 32 buildings that form a pattern. Use guidelines if necessary. To explore this further, you can render this sketch using different values with your markers to emphasize certain elements or continue to mirror your group of buildings vertically and horizontally to create an even larger pattern.

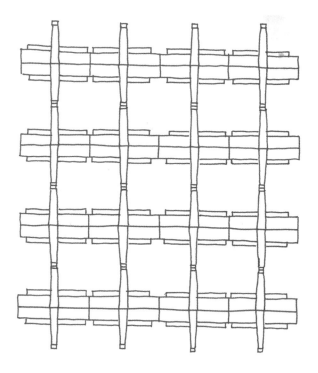

9.

Block out your building, indicating the centerline, and sketch one side, adding more architectural detail.

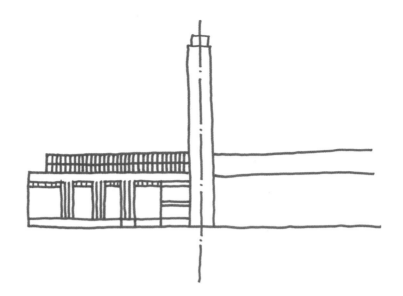

10.

Draw both sides, looking closely at your building and your sketch. Although the building itself is symmetrical, it is likely that the surrounding features will not be. In this example the Millennium Bridge (by Foster + Partners) approaches the museum on the left side of the viewer. The bridge and the trees add context and asymmetry to the sketch, providing a more realistic view of urban life than the symmetrical building in isolation (for more on landscape see the Vegetation exercise, page 114).

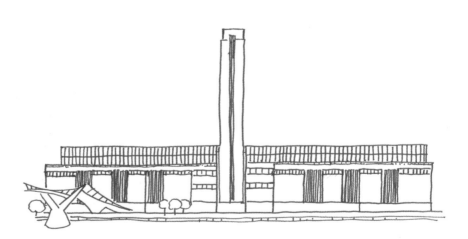

BUILDING SPECIFICATION

Tate Modern
Herzog & de Meuron I London, UK I 2000

PUZZLE PIECES

1.

Select a building composed of individual pieces Abstract the building you have chosen into simple shapes. Give each shape a number according to its proximity to the viewer—starting at 1 for the closest and rising to 5 for the farthest.

This exercise uses abstraction to study the sculptural qualities of a building. We examined abstraction in previous exercises as a tool to use for subjects from small (furniture) to medium (interiors), and now we will apply it to a larger scale (buildings). Applying this concept to the study of buildings is beneficial, especially with complex or irregular forms. In this example a modern addition (right) contrasts with the symmetry of the original building (left)—accentuated by the addition's many angular, irregular forms, making it ideal to pull apart and examine. Examining elements of a building in different ways allows the viewer to experience the architecture from a different mindset.

2.

Render the shapes with gray markers from darkest to lightest, as they recede from the viewer

3.

Draw the pieces as individual shapes.

4.

Draw the shapes as puzzle pieces; mix
them up to create an abstract drawing.
This is a fun way to explore the shapes
and look at them in a new way. Repeat
this two more times.

5.

Render the pieces with the assigned
values.

6.

Draw your building with architectural
detail. In this example the newer addition
is attached to (and appears to have
crashed into) the older building, so
it is important to add details to both
buildings even if the focus is on
the modern addition.

BUILDING SPECIFICATION

Royal Ontario Museum
Daniel Libeskind I Toronto, Canada I 2007

NEGATIVE SPACE

This exercise focuses on the space around a building. As stated in previous exercises, paying attention to negative space is a key aspect of sketching. The focus on the negative or void strengthens the perception of the form and can be examined in many ways—as a line, a shape, or a solid hatch around a building. In this example the many angles of the building provide a unique study of negative space and are used to further explore these ideas.

1.

Select a building with an interesting form With your thick pen, draw a line around the perimeter of your object. Focus on the outside edge of the form to create an outline of the overall exterior shape.

2.

With the thin tip of your black marker, use a tight squiggle to render the space around your building.

3.

With the thin tip of your black marker, use a loose squiggle to render the space around your building.

4.

Draw an invisible box around your
building, and sketch the shapes that
occur between your building and the box.

5.

Render the shapes with varied gray
values to provide contrast.

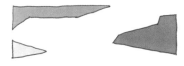

6.

Use the thick end of one of your gray
markers to create a loose, sketchy
rendering that represents the void
around your building.

7.

Sketch the building in its entirety,
focusing on the negative space to draw
the architectural forms.

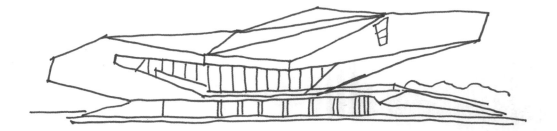

BUILDING SPECIFICATION

EYE New Dutch Film Institute
Delugan Meissl Associated Architects I
Amsterdam, Netherlands I 2011

EXPRESSION

A building can be expressed in many ways; your interpretation is unique. Depending on the building and the way it makes you feel, you may produce a very serious sketch or something more loose and playful. This exercise explores the notion of studying a building and bringing out the energy of the architecture. After you complete the exercise—quick sketches to slower drawings, loose strokes to tighter lines, and less detail to highly detailed elements—ask yourself which sketch best expresses your interpretation of the building and captures the feeling of the architecture.

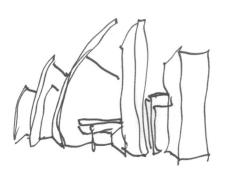

1.

Select a building with a sense of movement Use your thick pen to create a quick sketch of your building, using your left hand if you are right-handed or your right hand if you are left-handed. The beauty of this exercise is the focus on the building; there are no expectations for the final result. In this example the curves in this church create energy, and the loose sketch captures the expression of the architecture.

2.

Sketch and fill in the forms of your building quickly, using the thick tip of your black marker.

3.

Use the thick tip of your black marker again to quickly outline the building forms in broad strokes.

4.

Create another sketch with the thick tip of your marker, spending more time on defining the forms and the building detail.

5.

Use the thin tip of your black marker to create a loose sketch that gives more architectural detail to your building.

6.

With your thick pen, draw the building with more detail.

7.

Using your medium pen, spend the time you need to create a final sketch that defines and details all aspects of the architecture.

BUILDING SPECIFICATION

Jubilee Church

Richard Meier I Rome, Italy I 2003

BUILDING MATERIALS

Rendering the materials of a building adds another level of information to an architectural sketch. This exercise provides initial practice representing common materials used in the exterior of buildings, such as wood, stone, and concrete. These materials are then applied in context, to a multi-gabled house.

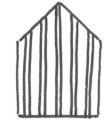
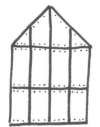

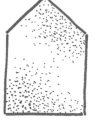
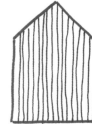

1.

Draw 12 squares (or the outline of a simple house, as seen here). Render each shape with a different building material. Use the materials in this example or create your own. Alternate between your medium and thin pens, exploring how the different pens change the representation of the material. Materials rendered with a thin pen are more subtle and do not distract from the form of the building, but there may be instances when you want the material to read more dominantly, in which case you would use a medium or thick pen.

The renderings in this example represent:

(top) textured wood; smooth stone; wood shingles; rough stone

(center) clapboard wood; concrete; wood, metal, or vinyl; wood strips of varied length

(bottom) brick; stucco; corrugated aluminum; uneven stone

2.

Select a building Study and draw your building as a line drawing.

3.

Render each element of your building using a different building material.

4.

Draw your building and render it in the actual building material used.

BUILDING SPECIFICATION

Fletcher House
Hugh Newell Jacobsen I Nashville, Tennessee, USA I 2003

BUILDING LAYERS

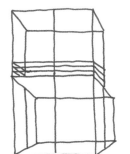

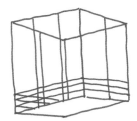

Previously we have used the term layering to refer to the overlapping elements in a perspective sketch. In this exercise we will take layering more literally, and peel back the actual physical layers of a building. By understanding the different components that make up the exterior of a building and studying them as unique architectural elements, you will gain a better understanding of the building as a whole.

1.

Select a building Draw the outermost layer of the building you select. In this example the thin framework that creates the structure and handrails of the porch/balcony at the rear of the house are expressed first.

2.

Peeling away the layer previously sketched, draw the next layer. The abstract arrangement of the multi-size windows is shown.

3.

Create a sketch of the next layer—in this example, the horizontal siding that covers the building.

4.

After your layers are peeled away, you will be left with the basic form of your building. Draw this form.

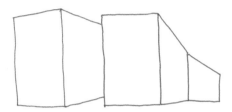

5.

Now that you have a deeper understanding of the layers of your building, draw your building in its entirety. If you are working in ink (and will not be able to erase), begin with the layer that is closest to you and sketch the layers in the order that they recede.

BUILDING SPECIFICATION

Y House
Steven Holl I Catskills, New York, USA I 1999

BUILDING LEVELS

We explored the physical layers of the Y House, but layers also occur in large-scale buildings. This exercise looks at horizontal layering that occurs—most often in tall buildings. When drawing a building of this type, it is important to examine the floor levels and gain an understanding of the overall structural grid of the architecture. In this example two 16-story towers located side by side share the same architectural language.

1.

Select a tall building Create a diagram indicating the ground, floors, and roofline of your building, and label them using four-floor increments.

2.

Use the thick side of your marker to emphasize every other floor level.

3.

Block out and sketch a basic drawing of the building, emphasizing the floor levels.

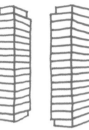

4.

Draw your building in parts, emphasizing the three basic elements of a tall building or skyscraper—the base (bottom), shaft (middle), and crown (top).

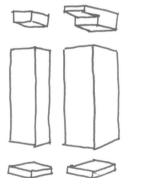

5.

Draw the parts together as a whole, showing the floor levels to create a sketch that combines the floor lines with more architectural detail of the building.

6.

Add the vertical elements of the building, such as the glass curtain-wall structure.

7.

Draw your building within its surrounding context. Through the towers, one can glimpse the Empire State Building, as well as a variety of other buildings and rooftops. Although drawn with less detail than the towers, these contextual buildings and trees emphasize the layered complexity of the city.

8.

Using markers, render an element of your building that you want to emphasize. In this example the glass is rendered with a 70 per cent gray value to contrast against the white balconies. This makes the buildings stand out from the urban background and provides greater definition.

BUILDING SPECIFICATION

173/176 Perry Street
Richard Meier | New York, USA | 2002

LEFT-TO-RIGHT PERSPECTIVE

In the Furniture + Lighting and Interiors sections, we explored perspective—including the idea that all elements within a view that fall along an orthogonal line recede to a VP. This is nowhere more evident than in architecture, where the larger scale allows you to understand this principle in a more profound way. If you view a building while walking from one end of a street to the other end, you will slowly see the perspective change and the VPs shift from the side of the building to behind the building, and to the other side. This exercise examines these subtle changes and records three points along your path. In this example the abstracted block forms of the architecture create interesting geometric views at each designated point.

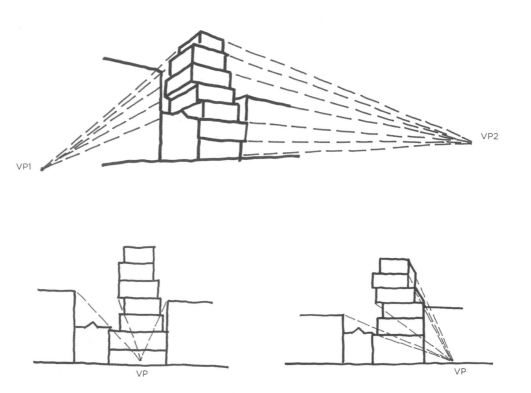

1.

Select a building that you can view from three points Start with the first point along your path. Indicate your VPs, and dash the lines that radiate out from the VPs to your building and surrounding buildings (if applicable). Sketch the basic forms of your building using your thick pen. Repeat with two other points along your path.

2.

Select one of your views to render with markers, showing the elements closer to the ground (and the viewer) darker, and the elements as they recede from the viewer lighter. While many of the interior perspectives we have created recede into the distance horizontally, tall urban buildings recede into the distance vertically. Depending on the location of the viewer and height of the building, some buildings will also recede toward a VP above the building; this is the third point in a three-point perspective, which we will explore in the Multi-point Perspective exercise (see page 106). Here we will just use the gray values to produce the faded or ombré effect of a tall building receding up toward the sky.

3.

Complete a final sketch for each view along your path. In this example details such as signage/artwork and taxicabs give identity and a metropolitan frame of reference.

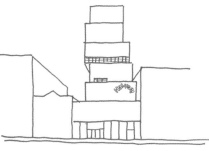
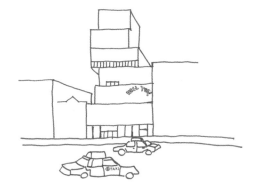

BUILDING SPECIFICATION

New Museum of Contemporary Art
SANAA I New York, USA I 2007

1.

Select a building with curved elevation(s) With your thick pen, draw your buildings from a two-point perspective (looking at the corner). At this stage treat the buildings as if they were rectilinear. Indicate and note your VPs with dashed lines that extend from the solid lines of your building outlines.

BUILDING CURVES

Sketching a building with curved elements requires the same basic approach you would use for a rectilinear building, but with a few additional tools. These structures evoke movement and fluidity, and your sketch should reflect that. This exercise builds upon the perspective methodology that we have previously studied. The two buildings chosen for this example highlight different aspects of portraying architectural curves.

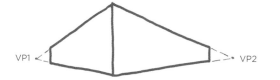

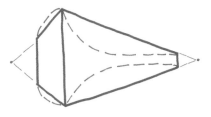

2.

Study the forms of your buildings and draw the curved lines on the elevations in dashes with your medium pen. The building on the left has one curved elevation (that curves within the drawn outline) and one rectilinear elevation. The house on the right is in the form of a crescent. Therefore, looking at the house from the corner one can see the outer, convex curve extending outside of the outline on the left of the corner, while the inner, concave curve on the right of the corner remains inside the outline.

3.

Draw the outline of your buildings
without guidelines. Continue to practice
as necessary to achieve a curve with
a smooth, consistent line.

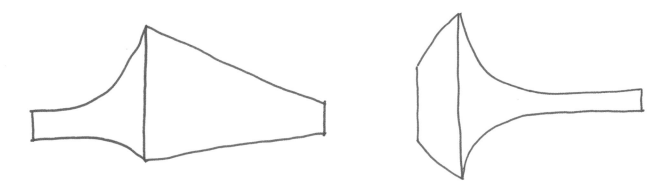

4.

Draw your buildings with architectural
and exterior detailing, including sidewalk
paving, exterior steps, and vegetation.

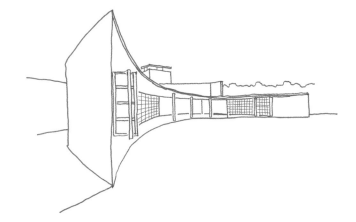

BUILDING SPECIFICATIONS from left

Trinity Laban Conservatoire of Music & Dance
Herzog & de Meuron I London, UK I 2003

Crescent House
Make Architects I Wiltshire, UK I 2000

MULTI-POINT PERSPECTIVE

For most of this book, the focus has been on understanding and mastering one- and two-point perspective views in sketches. As discussed, one-point views occur when you are looking directly at a building, and two-point views occur when you have an angled view of a building, toward an edge or a corner, for example. However, there are many buildings that incorporate more than two VPs. This can be seen in buildings with complex rooflines, or more modern buildings that incorporate uncommon forms. This exercise will examine three-point perspective drawings, looking up or down at a building, as well as more complex buildings that have four or more VPs when viewed from the standard 5-foot eye level.

The five principles of three-point perspective:

1. Two of the VPs are located on the horizon line.
2. The third VP is located above the horizon line (if you are looking up) or below the horizon line (if you are looking down).
3. All lines recede to a VP (there are no horizontal or vertical lines).
4. All objects get smaller as they recede into the distance.
5. All objects will become foreshortened, since all objects are located on orthogonal lines.

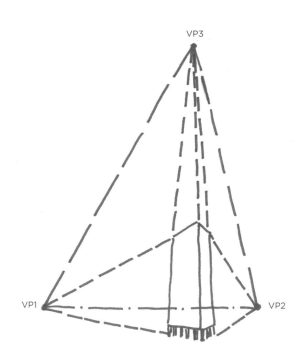

1.

Part 1: Select a tall building Sketch your building from a three-point perspective, looking up at the building. Show your dashed lines and indicate the location of the VPs.

2.

Sketch the building quickly with a thick pen, adding more architectural detail.

3.

Sketch the building from a three-point perspective, looking down at the building. In reality, you may not be able to view your building from above, but you can use the skills learned to imagine the view from this angle. Show your dashed lines and indicate the location of the VPs.

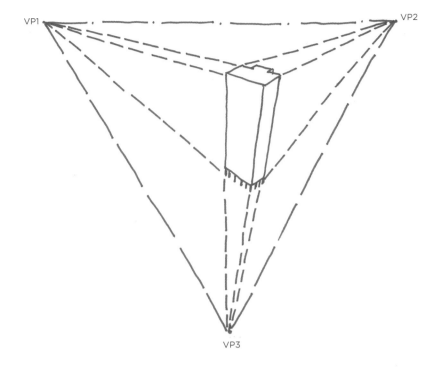

VP1

VP2

VP3

4.

Sketch the building quickly with a thick pen, adding more architectural detail.

BUILDING SPECFICATION

Seagram Building
Mies van der Rohe I New York, USA I 1958

5.

Part 2: Select a building with multiple VPs Outline and extend the basic forms of your building to their respective VPs. Label the elements and the VPs as 1, 2, 3, etc., to indicate what element recedes to what point. This building takes the basic house form but uses it in a novel way, which creates a separate VP for each element of the house.

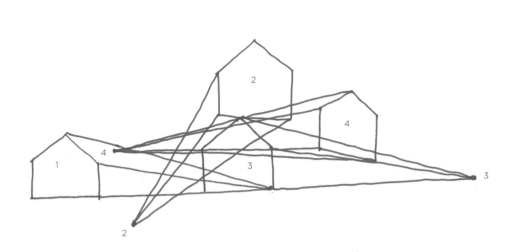

6.

To simplify the confusing nature of multiple VPs, render each element with a different value of gray.

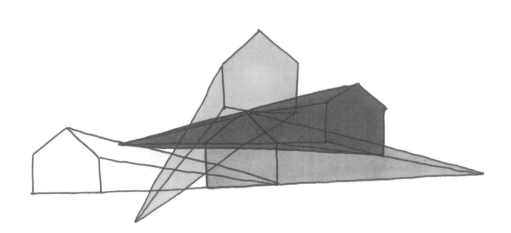

7.

Draw your building, using your
perspective study as a tool.

BUILDING SPECFICATION

VitraHaus
Herzog & de Meuron I Weil am Rhein,
Germany I 2010

PERIMETER VIEWS

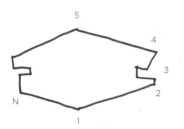

1.

Select a building with varied, interesting elevations Create a map of the building by outlining the overall plan view and labeling the different sides/views that you will sketch, starting at 1 and moving around the building. It is good practice, wherever possible, to indicate the direction of north on a building/floor plan.

A key principle of modernism is that a building must be explored from all angles to be appreciated fully. A classical building with a dominant front elevation is understood from one viewpoint; however, to understand a modern building in its totality, one must walk around the perimeter of the exterior and study each elevation closely. In this example an angled building (one that does not have traditional flat elevations) creates an interesting study. From the front elevation the viewpoint changes significantly as the viewer moves even just a few feet from right to left.

2.

Create a thumbnail sketch of your elevation from each of the views you have noted on your plan, starting with view 1. Above each sketch, draw the overall plan of the building and rotate it to indicate the view drawn. Use dashed lines to show the view of the building you have included in each sketch. The point where the two dashed lines meet indicates the location of the viewer at that particular view.

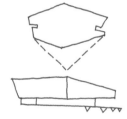

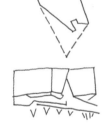

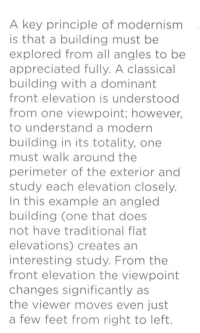

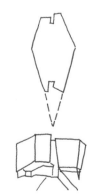

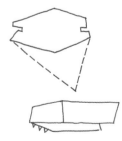

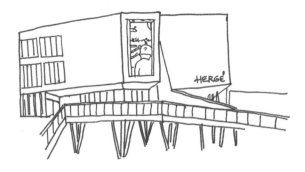

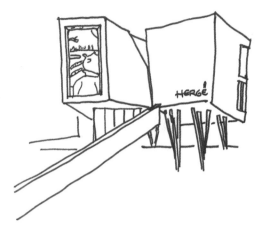

3.

Select three of your thumbnail views and
work them up into more detailed
architectural sketches.

BUILDING SPECIFICATION

Hergé Museum
Christian de Portzamparc I Louvain-la-Neuve,
Belgium I 2009

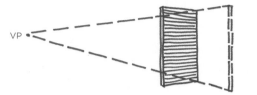

1.

Select a building with a moving element
Practice drawing the moving panel (in this case, a door). Draw the panel closed and render its material of construction (in this case, slatted wood). Then outline the panel in the open position. Mark the dashed lines that recede to your VP.

OPEN + CLOSED

Some buildings are radically transformed by the opening and closing of a moving panel such as a door, shutter, or window, changing the overall feel of the interior space and the appearance of the exterior. These mechanisms generally move on a hinge, pivot, or track—effecting a change from closed/dark to open/light. This exercise examines such elements, specifically how to detail a moving panel in perspective. The example chosen is a house that incorporates oversized panels which open and close. These will be analyzed individually and then explored within the larger context of the building.

2.

Draw your panel again in the closed position with the open position dashed. Draw a dashed curved line from the top corner of your closed panel to the top corner of your open panel. Draw some imaginary panels at different increments along your curved line to show the panel moving from closed to open.

3.

Draw your panel again in the closed position. Render the ghost panels from dark to light, with the darkest value used for the position at which the panel comes closest to the viewer.

4.

Draw your view three times, with
the panel in the open, half-open,
and closed positions.

 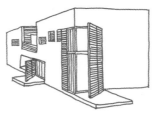 

5.

Draw the panel in isolation in each of the
three positions: open, half open, and
closed. Render the panel using a dark
value for closed, a medium value for half
open, and a light value for open.

6.

Using previous skills learned, render your
three sketches showing the exterior
building materials. In this example a light
pen was used to render the horizontal
multi-length strips of wood.

BUILDING SPECIFICATION

Box House
Maya Lin I Telluride, Colorado, USA I 2006

VEGETATION

Incorporating surrounding landscaping—trees and other vegetation—in your sketch gives context to your building and makes a cityscape dynamic. In this exercise we will explore various ways to draw vegetation, ranging from the realistic to the abstract, and then apply these styles to a building sketch. This example uses a building shaded by two large deciduous trees.

1.

Create a ground line with the thin tip of your black marker. Sketch approximately seven or eight deciduous trees in different drawing styles, from a simple lollipop to an intricate representation with branches and sub-branches. Include trees at different stages of their annual leaf cycle.

2.

Create another ground line with your black marker. Draw seven or eight more trees, a combination of evergreens (which keep their leaves all year round) and palm trees (useful for drawings of buildings in warmer climates). You can also create your own ways to draw trees and explore drawing bushes, flowers, and other vegetation.

3.

Select a building set among one or two large deciduous trees. Draw your building and the trees as they appear in your view. Then, draw your building showing the trees as they would appear at different times of the year. This example shows a winter view (top left), a spring view (top right), a summer view (bottom left), and a fall view (bottom right).

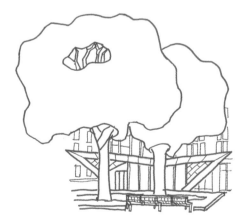

BUILDING SPECIFICATION

City of London Information Centre
Make Architects | London, UK | 2007

BUILDING SHADING

When drawing furniture and interiors, we are able to use artificial light sources to create shade and cast shadows as we desire. When sketching outside, we must rely on natural light to provide the shading and shadows. This means that if we want to understand the effects of light on an exterior, we have to visit the building at different times of the day to record what occurs as the position of the sun moves. In this exercise you will study a building throughout the day to explore the effect of the sun on the building and the unique shading and shadows that occur. This building was selected for its pure, minimalist form, which shifts the focus of the sketch to the light and the shadows that result.

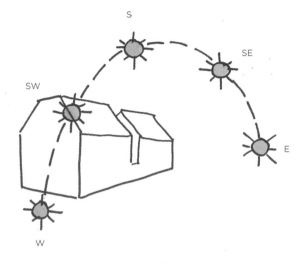

1.

Select a small, simple building Sketch the basic form of your building. On your sketch, block out and draw with dashes the path of the sun—as it rises in the east (E) and moves southeast (SE), south (S), southwest (SW), and finally sets in the west (W). To gain a deep understanding of the movement of the sun and the implications of shadow, you will need to visit your building five times during the day: in the early morning, late morning, early afternoon, late afternoon, and early evening.

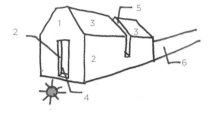

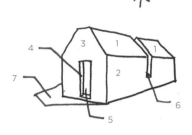

2.

Create a thumbnail of your building at each of your five points of the day. On each sketch code the areas of light and shade, using the number 1 for the brightest areas, and add an image of the sun to indicate its position in the sky (and, therefore, the time of day). Mark both the shading on the surfaces of the building and the shadow cast on the ground.

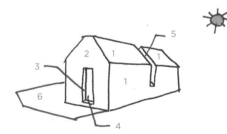

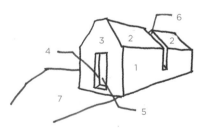

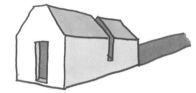

3.

Draw each building and render the planes as indicated by the numbers on your thumbnail sketches (for value 1, leave the white of the paper).

4.

Draw the building within its context. This stone house was originally exhibited within a colonnaded courtyard.

5.

Select one (or all) of your studies from the previous stage and use markers to render your contextual drawing. Apply shade to the surroundings according to the time of day represented in the drawing.

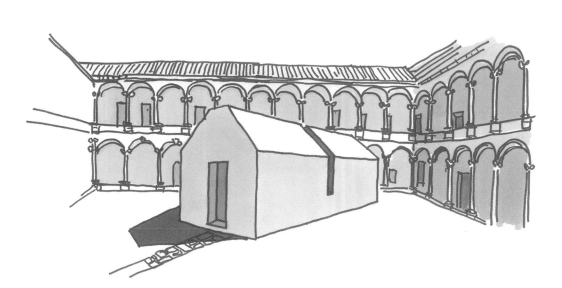

BUILDING SPECIFICATION

House of Stone
John Pawson I Milan, Italy I 2010

FINAL STUDY

This final exercise brings together many of the concepts from the three main chapters of this book. It is a condensed summary designed to give you the tools to study a building before sketching it in architectural detail. The six steps are easy to remember and are generally fairly quick to sketch, which makes the exercise especially useful for on-site sketches. The exercise includes practise of the following tools: abstracting a building into simple forms; looking at the building not the paper (thereby valuing the process over the end result); zooming in on a detail; including the surrounding context; and incorporating shade/shadow. The buildings in this example were selected for their strong, dominant forms and urban locations.

1.

Select three diverse buildings Study the pure, abstract forms and basic geometry of each building and draw the individual elements, focusing on the relationships between each form.

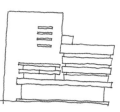

2.

Sketch with your eyes focused on the buildings, without looking at the paper. This is the technique we used in the Sculptural Study exercise (see page 70) to draw a stair and ceiling. It is a very good way to focus your attention on the form of the building itself, rather than on what the drawing looks like.

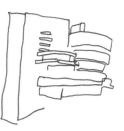

3.

Zoom in and draw a particularly
interesting detail of each building.
Exploring a detail in a larger scale
encourages you to reflect on the
architect's concept and design
intent, and promotes an intimate,
investigative process.

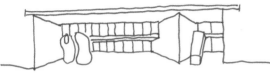 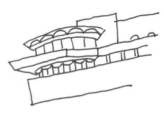 

4.

Draw the buildings in their totality—
mindful of the power of the line, of the
way that different forms connect to,
and interact with, each other, and of the
negative space that results. Consider
the effect of different levels of detail.

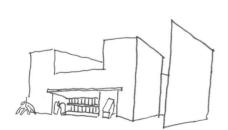  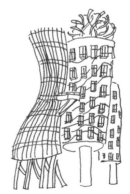

5.

Draw the buildings in context, whether rural, suburban, or urban. As previously discussed, buildings rarely stand in isolation—context plays an important role in their concept and design. Add elements such as surrounding buildings, vegetation, transportation, and people.

6.

Using the concepts of shade/shadow discussed throughout the book, study and determine the location of the sun, and shade the building and surroundings accordingly using your gray markers. These drawings incorporate many of the ideas and concepts in this book, and are a unique and personal interpretation of the buildings and their surroundings.

BUILDING SPECIFICATIONS from top

East Building at the National Gallery of Art
I. M. Pei I Washington, DC, USA I 1978

Solomon R. Guggenheim Museum
Frank Lloyd Wright I New York, USA I 1959

Nationale-Nederlanden Building
Frank Gehry and Vlado Milunic I Prague,
Czech Republic I 1996

THE AUTHOR

Stephanie received her Master of Architecture with distinction and Bachelor of Science in Architecture from the University of Michigan, Ann Arbor. She is currently the Director of the Interior Architecture and Design Program at The George Washington University (GW) in Washington, D.C. Prior to academia, she worked in New York City for Gensler and Vicente Wolf Associates, Inc. As an Associate Professor at GW, Stephanie focuses on studio courses in architectural design as well as sketching and the history of modern architecture and design. Her research focuses on design pedagogy and modern architecture. She has published articles and made presentations at national and international design conferences on these topics.

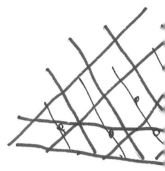

ACKNOWLEDGEMENTS

Thank you to Liz Faber, Peter Jones, Jon Allan, Laurence King, and the entire team at Laurence King Publishing Ltd. Extra thanks to Anna Galperin and Brooke Addams as well as my GW Interior Architecture + Design faculty. Thanks also to my husband Mark, daughter Samantha and son Matthew, and to my mom Judith, dad Alexander, and sister Michele for their support always.

Select content previously published in *The International Journal of Design Education*, Volume 7, Issue 3.